PRAISE FOR *ADVANCED CUSTOMER ANALYTICS*

'*Advanced Customer Analytics* provides a great introduction to the main analytical tools marketing managers should be familiar with. Starting from regression analysis, it gradually covers more sophisticated methods, including time series models, survival analysis, TOBIT models and structural equation models. What makes this book special is the easy-to-understand way in which these methods are explained and applied to problems marketing managers face every day. This makes this book great for practitioners as well as for readers interested in learning applied statistics. I strongly recommend this book to anyone interested in data-based marketing decision making.'
Michael Haenlein, Professor of Marketing, ESCP Europe

'This book gives the reader a truly enjoyable, very user-friendly explanation of several advanced techniques needed to assess marketing performance in the retail industries. It is written clearly enough for non-statisticians, but the analytics, with applications and results, are unerring, appropriate and educational in those areas that many retail managers and executives need to get up to speed with.'
Mike Morgan, President and CEO, Morgan Analytics Inc

'This book is a great one. It bridges the gap between theory and practice of statistics in the field of marketing and vividly illustrates how analytics can direct business strategy and decision optimization. It covers the full spectrum of marketing analytics... from demand forecasting through elasticity modelling, customer segmentation, campaign selection optimization through campaign measurements. I recommend this book to all students, analysts and marketing managers.'
Delali Agbenyegah, Predictive Analytics Manager, Alliance Data Card Services

'Written from a practice viewpoint, *Advanced Customer Analytics* is an engaging and easy-to-read book that will interest students and practitioners attentive to research and, more specifically, retailing. The book is conceptually substantial and serves as a practical guide to understanding and applying retail analytics. A particular strength of the book is the application to relevant industry issues facing large retailers today (such as Wal-Mart, Sears, Macy's, Kohl's, etc) as more and more companies are facing downsizing and restructuring pressures.'
Dr Candice R Hollenbeck, PhD, University of Georgia, Terry College of Business

'Mike Grigsby, author of *Marketing Analytics: A practical guide to real marketing science*, takes a critical and in-depth look at the issues under-pinning customer analytics. This book provides a fresh and comprehensible view on the complex issue of advanced customer analytics. Starting from the basics of regression and factor analysis, it quickly moves to what is essential in business and marketing, ie purchasing, order of purchases, pricing and discounts, allocation of marcomm, bundling, category management and CLV. The book is full of practical examples from the retailing industry, such as how to use Latent Class Analysis for segmentation (sounds fancy but don't worry you will learn it later) and more importantly it shows how the analysis is actually extremely helpful. If you want to deepen your knowledge of customer-focused analytics this is the book to read!'
Jari Salo (DSc), Professor of Marketing (Digital Business and Marketing), Oulu Business School

'Mike Grigsby has once again presented complex marketing concepts in a way that will enable newcomers to the field to appreciate the fundamental rationale economics plays in carrying out good market research. The reader is guided through the appropriate use of many popular statistical procedures to address basic marketing concerns. The author's no-nonsense (and at times humorous) interpretation of statistical output provides an excellent template to help more seasoned marketing analysts explain their work. At the very least, the reader will enjoy a very entertaining discussion of the making of marketing analytics. I highly recommend *Advanced Customer Analytics*.'
Derek Glatz, Senior Pricing Analyst, Loewe-Adler International Inc

'This book is an extremely useful resource which gives a wide overview on targeting, segmenting and building, and on measuring customer loyalty in retailing. It presents a practical application of traditional techniques applied to different kinds of non-traditional data, helping practitioners to understand the basics of marketing analytics in retail.'
Professor Lina Anastassova, PhD, Head of Marketing Chair,
Burgas Free University, Bulgaria

'We are in the midst of digital business and society transformation. Also known as the real-time digital economy. Marketers past, present and future need to understand this world, how it will influence clients and customers and how analytics will optimize messaging for decision makers from all professional backgrounds. Mike Grigsby has been at the genesis of this tipping point for quite some time and, in this book, has captured many great methods and experiences to set you on this journey.'
Tony Hamilton, Solution and Best Practices Consultant, Planet Analytics

'Dr Grigsby has done it again! *Advanced Customer Analytics* provides practical approaches in an easy-to-understand, easy-to-apply manner, highlighting Dr Grigsby's expertise and talent for translating complex ideas with ease. Practitioners would be wise to equip themselves with this latest effort to help them make smarter, data-driven decisions on the job.'
Dr James A Mourey, Assistant Professor of Marketing, DePaul University

'Mike Grigby's style of writing is easy and straight to the point. In *Advanced Customer Analytics* he includes specific maths and statistics examples that are relevant and easy to follow. If you want to step up your analytics understanding then this book is for you.'
Emmett Cox, SVP Customer Intelligence, BBVA Compass and
author of *Retail Analytics*

ADVANCED CUSTOMER ANALYTICS

MIKE GRIGSBY

ADVANCED CUSTOMER ANALYTICS

Targeting, valuing, segmenting and loyalty techniques

MARKETING SCIENCE SERIES

First published in Great Britain and the United States in 2016 by Kogan Page Limited

2nd Floor, 45 Gee Street	MPHC Marketing	4737/23 Ansari Road
London EC1V 3RS	122 W 27th St, 10th Floor	Daryaganj
United Kingdom	New York NY 10001	New Delhi 110002
www.koganpage.com	USA	India

© Mike Grigsby, 2016

The right of Mike Grigsby to be identified as the author of this work has been asserted by him in accordance with the Copyright, Designs and Patents Act 1988.

A small amount of the content in this book has been published previously in Mike Grigsby's book *Marketing Analytics: A practical guide to real marketing science* (Kogan Page, 2015). Due to its close relevance to customer analytics, it has also been included here for the benefit of readers of this book.

ISBN   978 0 7494 7715 8
E-ISBN   978 0 7494 7716 5

British Library Cataloguing-in-Publication Data

A CIP record for this book is available from the British Library.

Library of Congress Cataloging-in-Publication Data

Names: Grigsby, Mike, author.
Title: Advanced customer analytics : targeting, valuing, segmenting and
   loyalty techniques / Mike Grigsby.
Description: London ; New York : Kogan Page, [2016] | Includes
   bibliographical references and index.
Identifiers: LCCN 2016033366 (print) | LCCN 2016040672 (ebook) | ISBN
   9780749477158 (alk. paper) | ISBN 9780749477165 (ebook)
Subjects: LCSH: Marketing research. | Customer relations. | Customer loyalty.
Classification: LCC HF5415.2 .G7539 2016 (print) | LCC HF5415.2 (ebook) | DDC
   658.8/12--dc23
LC record available at https://lccn.loc.gov/2016033366]

Typeset by Graphicraft Limited, Hong Kong
Print production managed by Jellyfish
Printed and bound by CPI Group (UK) Ltd, Croydon, CR0 4YY

CONTENTS

Datasets relating to chapters are available online at:
www.koganpage.com/Advanced-Customer-Analytics

OVERVIEW 01

Oh, so glad you dropped in. Thanks and I'll try to make it worth your while. In this Overview chapter we'll have a general introduction, which will help you know if you're in the right place or not. I know how you'd hate to waste your time.

What is retail?

This is about analytics focussing on retail and retail-ish firms, so let's define each term. There's a whole chapter on just what do I mean by retail but let's begin with the obvious: retail is an entity in the distribution chain, after manufacturing, after wholesale but before final consumption. That is, in traditional broad-based retail, I do not include manufacturers, I do not include wholesalers. They are a different ballgame, have different roles or purposes and face different (especially cost) pressures. The retail entity is that part of the distribution chain that takes from the wholesaler (who has taken goods from the manufacturer) and sells those goods to the final customer. These entities are mutually exclusive. (We'll ignore vertically integrated firms.) Simple, right?

So Apple is a manufacturer, even though it has stores that sell to a final customer. Honda is a manufacturer even though it has dealers that repair automobiles for the final customer. Neither of these is a retailer by definition. They do not waltz the double-edged dance of the cost of supply and factor inputs that traditional retailers tango with. Think of Wal-Mart, that has factor inputs, and sells a broad array of products and brands in each product to the final customer. Wal-Mart can use this book.

By retail I also mean an organization that has 'stores', a market and a place where buyers and sellers meet. This is a location that distributes the manufactured goods (or services) to final customers. Yes, this can be an online-only location but that has other unique issues. The idea is that a retailer has control over a market (where buyers and sellers meet) that allows the final customer to 'experience' the brand. There are grey areas of course but now you know what I mean by (strict) retail.

So what do I mean by retail-ish? This includes some of the grey areas but also those industries that are near retail. That is, hotels. They are not manufacturers/wholesalers and they have 'stores' wherein the final customer can experience their brand. So this book will work for them. I would also include dining as a retail-ish industry. Restaurateurs buy food items from manufacturers (farmers) and wholesalers to re-combine into a product/service for final customers in a multitude of stores/restaurants. See?

What is analytics?

Now, let's define analytics. Yes, it means something mathematical, more accurately, statistical. Analytics is that quantitative arm of (generally) marketing or operations that decreases the risk of making a wrong decision. It is fuelled by econometrics, marketing research, operations research, psychometrics, etc. It's basically where all the fun happens. This book will deal heavily with marketing science applications, and not much around financial/investment decisions. Note that this book should be viewed as a continuation (with some overlap) of my last book (*Marketing Analytics*, Kogan Page, 2015).

Who is this book for?

This book is for the practitioner, or those who soon hope to be practitioners. There is a lot about data and a lot about strategy, but it is aimed at the analytic practitioner. The practitioner that works in and around retail and retail-ish industries will get the most use from it. Not in manufacturing, wholesaling or utilities. Financial services? Barely. Medical services? Not really. Think of Wal-Mart and all Wal-Mart-like places (JC Penney, Sears, Macy's, Kohl's, Shopko) and you're in the right ballpark. Specialty retailers (such as Michaels, Best Buy, Toys R Us, Gap) are also a good fit.

Why focus on retail?

Good question. There are three primary reasons. First, retail is awash in data. Retail has all kinds of data, Big Data, little data, good data and easy data, more and more data. Data from POS systems, marcomm responses, overlay data, social media, marketing research, etc.

Also, retail is close to the customer. Retail listens to the customer, knows the customer. This means analytics get immediate feedback from projects and know instantly if something works. Or doesn't.

Lastly, retail tends to operate on thin margins and needs smart and intelligent decision-making to succeed. That means retail needs analytics more than other industries do.

Why am I making these suggestions?

My first job was in retail (shoes) and I've worked at Gap as well. I've been a consultant for many retail firms (including Famous Footwear, Best Buy, Fossil, Radio Shack, Shopko, Joann's Fabric and Craft, TGI Fridays and Papa Murphy's).

My background has been entirely in (marketing) analytics. For nearly 30 (gulp) years. I have worked in CRM, direct/database marketing, decision analysis, forecasting, website analytics, marketing research and all the ancillary positions supporting those functions. So I've been around. I've been a practitioner. This book is the result of all I have learned and believe over these decades.

I have also taught college courses (graduate and undergraduate) and have great sympathy and passion for those learning to do analytics. I think I have evolved toward a (strong) point of view on several topics and can speak with authority, not from mere academia but from in-the-trenches experience. I know these things work because I've seen them work. It is not always as the textbooks say and in the real world we have to use what works in practice.

How is this book organized?

Much like my last book, this one is around (typically marketing) questions. It is not necessarily designed to be read in sequence, except for the introductory chapters. Look at what you are trying to accomplish, look at what you are trying to answer, and find that chapter that will give analytic techniques in order to answer that question.

For example, 'How do I estimate demand?' is an important question. You're going to find out that there are two general kinds of analysis: dependent-type and interrelationship-type. The demand chapter (Chapter 5) will argue that since demand (units) is what you are trying to understand and whose movement you are trying to explain (that is, demand DEPENDS on other things), therefore a dependent-type technique is what's needed. Ordinary linear regression will be advocated and discussion will be around how to use regression, what to look out for, why it works, how to display it in practice, etc. Then there will be a business case involving the use of ordinary regression in explaining the problem of demand.

We will follow an analyst, Scott, whose job is to do what your job is to do: estimate demand. Scott's boss, for example, wants to know how impactful is advertising, or what is the relationship between price and units, or what can seasonality predict is coming, or any number of demand-like questions. You will be armed with ordinary regression and an example of how to apply it and an explanation of why it works.

OK, now on to a little background. Ordinary regression will be introduced as a dependent-type technique and factor analysis will be introduced as an interrelationship-type technique.

REGRESSION AND FACTOR ANALYSIS

02

An introduction

Introduction

You will need to have firmly in mind measures of central tendency (mean, media and mode), and measure of dispersion (range, variance and standard deviation). These are descriptive statistics on one variable. Of much more interest is statistics on two or more variables. These include covariance, correlation and R^2. It's very important that you are comfortable with z-scores, confidence intervals and t-tests.

This all too brief chapter will serve as a statistical overview. First let's define two types of thinking: deductive and inductive. Deductive reasoning is 'top down', and moves from general to specific items. It is the 'If-then-else' conclusion. Inductive reasoning is 'bottom up', and moves from specific to general items. It is the generalizing/extrapolating conclusion. Statistical analysis (while, for our purposes is ultimately about causality) is an inductive process. Statistics takes a sample and generalizes (and quantifies how safe that generalization is) to the population.

This is a good place to describe the three kinds of data and the uses of data. The first and simplest is *descriptive* data and analysis. This uses past data only, usually outputs descriptive statistics/metrics and is all about what happened. This is mathematic (at best) and not statistical. There is no probability statement attached. These usually include things like trends, descriptive statistics, KPIs, dashboards. The function that performs this is often called business intelligence (BI). This is a necessary but not sufficient analytic step.

The next stage in increasing complexity is *predictive* data and analysis. This book will live in the predictive stage. Predictive analysis is all about probability, estimating a change in one metric given a change in another metric. It is statistical and insightful.

The third stage is *prescriptive*. It is generally a system of equations and is a simulation. It is all about optimizing some metric (typically net profit, satisfaction, etc), given how one variable and equation impacts another variable and equation. This book will gently touch on this stage.

So this chapter will give a brief overview of the primary types of analytics we will cover. As mentioned in the Introduction there are two general types of statistical analysis: dependent variable-type and interrelationship-type. Regression is the prototypical dependent variable-type and factor analysis is the prototypical interrelationship-type. There are other dependent variable/equation types of analysis than ordinary regression: discriminate, conjoint (which uses regression), logistic regression and Cox regression (proportional hazards/survival modelling), and tobit amongst them. There are other types of interrelationship techniques including principal components and most importantly (to marketing analysis) segmentation. This chapter will start off on ordinary regression and exploratory factor analysis.

Regression 101: What is regression?

So, what is regression? Regression is a statistical analytic technique, indeed a dependent variable-/equation-type technique. Regression posits that a dependent variable DEPENDS upon one or more independent variables. It is usually of the form $Y = \alpha + \beta X$ where Y is the dependent variable and X is the independent variable(s). (A variable is a thing that varies.) Now this equation also has two constants (a thing that does NOT vary): α and β. The alpha α is the intercept or constant and the beta β is the slope or coefficient. Let's dive into these two parameters for a moment, as it is these constants that regression is trying to estimate.

Let's start by revisiting basic algebra, in particular the algebra of a straight line. Remember $Y = mx + b$, the equation of a straight line? Y is the dependent variable and X is the independent variable; b is the intercept and m is the slope. Sound familiar? Note how this is very similar to the regression equation. The concepts are the same. Regression is linear (in the parameters, β supplies the rise over run, or the average impact of X on Y) and that line will intersect on the vertical axis. Where it intersects is the 'intercept' and the impact is the 'slope'. Now, in algebra, every point of Y is exactly calculated by $mx + b$: it is the equation of a straight line. In statistics we have the concept of probability, a random error that also impacts the estimated dependent variable. So the whole expression is $Y = \alpha + \beta X + e$, where e is a random, unknown term. It is this e that causes all the trouble because we do not have an exactly calculated straight line. We have data on the actual dependent variable Y and the regression equation estimated a dependent variable that will get us 'close' to the actual dependent variable. The statistical question is, 'How close is close?' The answer is, it depends on the criteria.

Ordinary regression is also called ordinary least squares (OLS) because that is the criteria. The job of the algorithm is to estimate the parameters (α and β) in such a way to get the estimated dependent variable as close as possible (as often as possible) to the actual dependent variable. Now it turns out that there are an infinite number of lines that can be drawn through the points of a data series. Ordinary regression takes the rule to 'minimize the sum of squared errors' in calculating the parameters. Conceptually, the algorithm calculates the squared difference between each actual and predicted dependent variable and finds the intercept and slope that minimizes this summed difference. That's the rule: find the estimated parameters that minimize the sum of the squared errors. (The actual calculus behind this, the equations that result from this and proofs of this are in dozens of econometric textbooks, which we will not deal with here.)

So, why call this thing *regression*? Is something regressing, going backward? Yes. As a term it was invented by Francis Galton (taking from Gauss's earlier method of least squares). Galton noticed that tall people had children who tended to be shorter than they were. This tendency was towards a normal height. That is, children's height went back (regressed) to the population mean.

Assumptions of classical linear regression

You should be aware that regression comes with baggage. It is extremely powerful and gives great insights, but it comes with baggage. That is, the analyst must know what to do with it, how to use it and what it means. This requires an understanding of the tool and what it can and what it cannot do. That is, while a thermometer is a powerful tool it will not give insights into blood pressure.

This baggage is embedded in the assumptions of classical normal linear regression. In a very real way, econometrics is really about dealing with these assumptions: understanding these violations of assumptions, knowing how to diagnose and knowing how to correct, these violations of assumptions. These assumptions are listed in detail in any econometric textbook and are counted and detailed in several different ways. My treatment will be conceptual rather than statistical:

- **First Assumption: functional form** – the dependent variable is a linear function of the independent variables and an error term. Violations of these assumptions are wrong regressors, non-linearity and changing parameters. Consequences of violating this assumption are typically biased parameter estimates. Correction has to do with re-stating the equation to account for non-linearity.

- **Second Assumption: zero mean of the error term** – the expected value of the disturbance term is zero. Violation of this assumption causes a biased intercept. Consequences of violating this assumption are biased intercepts. Corrections typically include logarithmic transformations involving Cobb–Douglass-like functional forms, or frontier production functional forms.

- **Third Assumption: homoscedasticity** – the error terms all have the same variance. Consequences of violating this assumption include large variances of the standard errors of the parameter estimates. The beta coefficients themselves are unbiased. Diagnosing heteroscedasticity includes the Goldfeld–Quandt test and the White test. Corrections typically involve re-estimating the regression with transformed (weighted) independent variables.

- **Fourth Assumption: uncorrelated error terms** – the error terms are uncorrelated. Consequences of violating this assumption include biased standard errors, typically downward. The beta coefficients themselves are unbiased. Diagnosing auto/serial correlation involves the Durbin–Watson test (for an AR(1) process). Corrections typically involve re-estimating the regression with transformed independent variables usually using the Cochrane–Orcutt procedure.

- **Fifth Assumption: uncorrelated independent variable(s) and error terms** – the independent variable(s) and error terms are uncorrelated. This is ultimately about assuming independent variable(s) are fixed in repeated samples. Violations of this assumption account for estimation problems including simultaneous equations, autoregression and errors in variables. If the independent variables(s) are contemporaneously correlated with the error term the estimates are (asymptotically) biased. Consequences of violating this assumption include biased parameter estimates. Corrections typically involve re-estimating with instrumental variables, simultaneous equations, etc.

Why is regression important and why is it used?

So, what's the importance of regression? A couple of things, entirely bound up in the dependent variable technique. Regression outputs coefficients on independent variables. That is, it provides quantitative estimates of causality. Ultimately strategy is about a belief (or a guess) that THIS causes

THAT; eg a decrease in price causes an increase in units. Regression quantifies (moves beyond a guess) which independent variables significantly impact the dependent variable and to what extent.

This means that the independent variables (those that are deemed statistically significant) provide an estimated impact (whether positive or negative) on the dependent variable. This is both insightful and lucrative. To summarize: regression answers, 'Which independent variables are significant in explaining the movement of the dependent variable?' and 'In which direction do these independent variables move the dependent variable?' and 'By how much do these independent variables move the dependent variable?'

Now a quick note about the different kinds of regression. While regression is a dependent variable technique and is formulated as one or more equations, it comes in different flavours. The most common is ordinary regression but marketers are very involved with logistic regression. A fairly new kind of regression (to marketing) is survival analysis. All the above are single-equation techniques. Marketing can (and sometimes should) be modelled as a system of equations. System techniques include simultaneous equations, vector autoregression, instrumental variables and structural equation modelling (SEM). This book will deal with the above, and more, because regression is one of the most fun things you can do in the corporate world.

Factor analysis

The next overview will focus on a completely different kind of technique: interrelationship analysis. Factor analysis is the poster child of these kinds of techniques, although principal component analysis is a close second. For marketing, segmentation is the all-important interrelationship analysis.

In general, factor analysis is used to aggregate the interrelationships among a large number of variables in order to identify the common (underlying) factors. Factor analysis helps understand structure in the data. A factor is a way of summarizing variance between variables, ie a factor explains how several variables 'load' into a common factor. This tends to result in two agreeable properties: 1) a handful of factors (less than the number of variables) explain how many variables interrelate; and 2) the resulting factors are orthogonal (uncorrelated).

Exploratory vs. confirmatory factor analysis

Most uses of factor analysis are exploratory. As mentioned, factor analysis is about understanding structure in the data, often for the purpose of reducing the dimensionality of the data, ie decreasing the number of variables used in a model.

Confirmatory factor analysis is a stronger view and asserts that the analyst KNOWS something about the structure in the data. This approach is often designed as SEM and uses factors in a dependent variable equation method to measure (confirm) structure in the data. SEM has great uses in marketing and will be dealt with later.

Using factor analysis

Factor analysis is a kind of statistical technique that has several applications for marketing analytics. The point of factor analysis (for us) is to decrease the dimensions of the variance of all the independent variables. For example, instead of using X1–X7 as independent variables, we use instead Factor 1–Factor 4 which contains say 80 per cent of the variance of the above variables. There is a trade-off in that the impact each individual variable has is buried within a factor that contains the common variance of more than one independent variable. It does this through eigenvalues. An eigenvalue is a construct measuring the amount of variance the observed variables in a factor explains. Any factor with an eigenvalue greater than 1.00 explains more variance than a single observed variable.

A common use case is in building a regression model. We have seven independent variables: number of e-mails sent, number of direct mails sent, number of SMS sent, number of transactions, time between transactions, average discount used and average net price paid. The dependent variable is units. We KNOW each marcomm (marketing communications) vehicle is correlated with each other, and discount and price are correlated with each other, and transactions and time between transactions are (probably) correlated with each other. Independent variables that are (highly) correlated with each other cause collinearity problems (discussed later) but even conceptually you should understand that it is not efficient to have several variables essentially measuring the same thing. Factor analysis will extract the common variable into a construct so that mathematically each construct (factor) is UNcorrelated with each and every other factor.

If we run factor analysis on all seven variables the output is as shown in Table 2.1. This shows that Factor 1 contains the mutually exclusive variance of 5.05 variables, whereas Factor 2 contains 0.72 of a variable, and so on. Most analysts stop somewhere around using 70–90 per cent if possible. In this case that would mean up to Factor 3 (at 92 per cent).

TABLE 2.1   Factor analysis output

	Eigenvalue	Proportion	Cumulative
1	5.05	0.72	0.72
2	0.72	0.10	0.82
3	0.70	0.10	0.92
4	0.32	0.05	0.97
5	0.16	0.02	0.99
6	0.05	0.01	1.00
7	0.00	0.00	1.00

Table 2.2 shows the factor loadings. Note that Factor 1 is mostly about marcomm and transactions, Factor 2 is mostly about discount and price.

So, instead of running a regression as:

units = f(number of e-mails sent, number of direct mails sent, number of SMS sent, number of transactions, time between transactions, average discount used, average net price paid)

which have high collinearity, we run a regression as:

units = f(Factor 1, Factor 2, Factor 3)

A final and probably obvious comment is that factor analysis is the kind of interrelationship technique that is used in segmentation. Segmentation is very important in marketing and is typically NOT done via dependent variable-type techniques. More on that (MUCH more) later.

TABLE 2.2 Factor loadings

	Factor1	Factor2	Factor3	Factor4	Factor5	Factor6	Factor7
E-MAIL	0.96	−0.01	−0.19	−0.11	−0.04	−0.17	0.02
DIRMAIL	0.87	0.15	−0.34	0.15	0.30	0.03	0.00
SMS	0.58	0.71	0.40	−0.06	−0.01	0.00	0.00
#Tranx	0.72	−0.31	0.51	0.34	0.02	−0.02	0.01
TB Tranx	0.81	−0.31	0.25	−0.40	0.11	0.06	0.00
DISC	0.01	0.94	−0.21	0.07	−0.20	0.12	0.03
PRICE	−0.15	0.98	−0.14	0.02	−0.12	−0.01	−0.05

Conclusion

You've taken a brief tour of the two major analysis approaches: dependent variable types and interrelationship types. This sets the stage for all that follows.

Checklist

You'll be the smartest person in the room if you:

☐ Focus on the three types of data and analysis: descriptive, predictive and prescriptive.

☐ Remember that ordinary regression is a dependent variable-type analysis. That is, the whole point of regression is to explain the movement in some dependent variable.

☐ Keep in mind all of the different types of regression: ordinary, logistic, probit, Poisson, survival, which are single-equation techniques. There are also multi-equation techniques such as SEM, 2SLS, 3SLS.

☐ Remember that regression comes with baggage, a set of assumptions that, if violated, can produce biased or inconsistent results.

▶

☐ Use regression to its advantage: giving strategic levers to pull
    (ie independent variables that explain or cause the movement in
    the dependent variable).

☐ Point out that factor analysis is an interrelationship-type technique
    and concerned with how variables interrelate with one another.

☐ Have a solid feel for factor analysis (including principal components)
    vis-à-vis segmentation. Segmentation is a key marketing analytic
    procedure.

RETAIL

03

Industry uniqueness

Introduction to retail

What is retail? Retail is the last element in the distribution chain and touches (sells to/serves) final customers. That is the basic definition. In order to be a retailer a firm has to receive goods from multiple manufacturers/ wholesalers and productize them in a form for final customers. That is, the retailer has to deal with upstream as well as downstream functions.

The distribution chain starts with one or more manufacturers that flow products to one or more wholesalers that flow products to one or more final customers. A traditional retailer sells many brands from many manufacturers. In strict definitional terms, Apple stores, for example, are NOT traditional retailers – they sell only one brand. Neither are Honda dealerships. While they each sell to/serve final customers they each are manufacturers. Their 'store' sells only one brand.

Part of what makes a retailer unique is that it must manage factor inputs from different vendors/manufacturers (who each have a different cost/competitive structure and strategy) and make the subsequent distribution chain as efficient as possible. When dealing with only one brand (indeed typically its mother/corporate brand) a store does not run into negotiation issues, variances in the bargaining power of suppliers, different cultures and geographic issues. Then the traditional retailer must deal with final customers (and all that that means) maintaining products that the retailer itself does not manufacture/produce. But that's why we will deal with 'retail-ish' industries.

It must be pointed out that while the above is the 100-year-old definition of retail, many authors and retail experts are predicting a drastic change. In *The New Rules of Retail*, for instance, Lewis and Dart predict the collapse of the distribution chain as detailed above. They advocate a focus on digital/online/social and customer-centric changes that will evolve the value chain into something else, certainly something LESS formal than manufacturers–wholesalers–retail stores–customers.

While it's hard to say at this stage just what will happen, it will still be true that the retail firm will get products and will be the middleman for selling products. In some ways, a better definition of the retailer might be 'the middleman' between the supplier and the demander. After all, the word 'retailer' comes from Old French meaning 'to cut off' and sell in small pieces. That is, transfer goods from raw material to finished product, from manufacturer to customer.

The retail industry is huge. Generally, 25 per cent of US jobs are in retail and there are nearly four million retail establishments generating nearly US$ 3 trillion. Retail is a strong focus for small business as over 98 per cent have fewer than 50 employees. Total retail sales growth is seen as a leading economic indicator and for the last few years has been about 4 per cent over the time period. Clearly the retail industry is an important and complex one worthy of analysis.

Brief history of retail

Retail is big and important and as such fairly recent in economic history. Yes, there have always been 'middlemen', those between the suppliers and the (final) consumers and that middleman can be called 'retailer'.

But for the last 100 years or so the history of retail industry has exploded and specialized. It was retail that took over agriculture as the driver of larger economies.

The early 1900s were dominated by mom-and-pop stores, dry goods and corner locations. The owner knew his customers and provided personalized services. Everything the owner did was customer-centric, even though assortment was limited and the store was general.

The department giants were the next evolutionary rung as the automobile made walking to the corner store unneeded. These giants (eg Sears, JC Penney) were VERY BIG, stocked everything, and the experience was nearly overwhelming. At about this time refrigerators became available so consumers could buy more, that is, store more.

Then huge department stores began to 'anchor' malls, which were centres of the shopper's galaxy. These malls could support many boutique and niche stores because of the giant traffic the big-box anchors brought in. These malls hosted cooperatives wherein many 'little guys' could pay a lease and all stores could drive traffic to all other stores. The consumer was happy because only one location was necessary for nearly all of these shopping needs. The technological invention was now the television, which could mass advertise and bring in yet more traffic.

The next wave of retail and technology brought about the value players (Wal-Mart, K-Mart, etc) and category killers (Toys R Us, Michaels). These next-generation retailers competed really only on price. The value players bought massive amounts of product at a volume discount and had such bargaining power over suppliers that they could demand a low cost of goods sold. They were then able to price in such a way to attract 'everyday low price' seekers.

The category killers strategized differently. They would buy up nearly every product within an associated category. While they had clout to dictate pricing the real consumer appeal was that shopping for a category meant it would be found there. That is, if a consumer was looking for some kind of toy, it would be found at Toys R Us, because they had everything.

The mid-90s changed everything, again. This saw the development of the internet and suddenly consumers could buy online. They had been able to buy over the telephone for some time but that made 'browsing' not an option. They had to talk to a customer service rep who was trying to sell them something. The internet made private shopping (browsing) possible.

Of course that paved the way for where we are now, with digital and social communities. Now consumers can share their experiences, blog and make positive or negative mentions of the stores or products. This means retailers have to pay attention more than ever.

It also means that retailers no longer have to be outbound marketers only (via direct mail and e-mail and SMS) but can rely on inbound marketing. That is, some of their customers have a lot of influence and have a lot of friends and contacts. These influencers can be used to aid in retailing, they can be recruited to use word of mouth and evangelize a retailer's strategy, experience, and products.

Retail analytics

Retail analytics has traditionally been stuck mostly in the descriptive phase. Because it moves so fast and is so close to the end user (customer) most retail leaders just want a pulse on the business and then scramble with ways to counteract the current effects. That is, they usually just react (and even panic) with short-sighted almost desperate actions, often involving cutting the price of products in order to pull in more revenue now (at the expense of the future) to salvage the current month or quarter. Thus a heavy reliance is on dashboards and key performance indicators (KPIs) and NOT on understanding and estimating cause and effect.

It's almost impossible to get retailers to do a true universal control group (UCG). That is, to withhold some statistically sound number of customers and NEVER promote to them. Even though the UCG will give them a true measure of incrementalism, they are very hesitant to remove ANY potential customers from communications. They usually demand this count be so small that it is impossible to statistically measure the lift other communications generate over a virgin test cell.

It is even very difficult to get retailers to engage in a simple A/B test, because that would mean taking out of circulation some stimuli, that is, the test portion of the cell design would NOT get the typical business as usual treatment.

Therefore, to actually take the time to collect data and design a predictive model and test it in the field is anathema to their culture. Many (especially merchandizers) actually fight the use of predictive analytics, especially from a marketing point of view. Unfortunately, it's true that in many retail organizations and cultures, marketing is the barely tolerated problem child.

Merchandizers just want marketers to 'fill the top of the funnel' and get customers into the stores, and then merchandizers will take it from there. So for marketers to advocate elasticity modelling to better target discounts will meet with protests that messing with prices will counter the merchandizer's product inventory or other forecasts.

Orientation: because retail is... this book is...

Let's orient the focus of this book, especially in terms of retail. This is a book about how analytics generates insights for strategic actions in the retail industry. By 'analytics' is meant marketing, operational and financial analysis. As such, several philosophic conceptions are followed:

1 **Because retail** is close to the final customer, this book will be customer-centric.

In order to apply a customer-centric approach some definitions need to be asserted. A CONSUMER is any person. A PROSPECT is a person known to the firm, typically having submitted say an e-mail address, but they are not a customer, they have not purchased from the firm. A CUSTOMER is a person whom we know and who has purchased from the firm. Many retailers make a further distinction between customer and active customer. That is, a non-active customer (called derisively 'deadwood') is a customer that has not purchased in a long time, say over a year.

The source of all retail strategy must have the focal point of customer-centricity. (While acquisition has its place, it is not typically in the top 10 retail strategies.) Everything that is done is ultimately about understanding and incenting and changing customer behaviour. This is a marketing conception. In marketing the customer is king, central to all that is undertaken.

That is, if the customer is understood, the firm can levy the marketing mix (product, price promotion and place) in such a way to create compelling messages and offers. Meaning that the customer nearly feels like a 'segment of one' and that the firm understands each particular customer so well that the firm takes on nearly monopoly power, ie becomes a price maker, rather than merely a price taker.

2 **Because retail** is focussed on product categories this book advocates a category management approach.

A product hierarchy is the bedrock of retail inventory management. Typically, merchandizers rule the retail world. They are responsible for buying and selling products (broad products are called categories) over a month, over a quarter etc. In retail, buying inventory (which has a financial depreciation) and forecasting the 'stock out' is critical to success. While this book will tend to have a marketing approach, it must be noted that, for retail firms to thrive, a good method to forecast inventory must be operationally effective. This should be a multi-disciplinary approach.

3 **Because retail** is last in the distribution chain (after manufacturers, wholesalers) this book seeks to understand the customer (causality) mindset.

While this is again part of the marketing concept no merchandizer or operations analyst would ignore customer behaviour, tastes and preferences. Again, customer behaviour is central.

A lot of analytics seeks to quantify causality. 'This causes that' is the application of deductive reasoning, even though most statistical analysis uses inductive reasoning. Thus the understanding of customer behaviour is fully analysed.

4 **Because retail** is about impulse buying this book spends a lot of effort on elasticity modelling and discount strategies.

Retailers know they send too many discounts and offer too many promotions and give away too much margin. But they typically do not have an analytic way to target or predict different price sensitivities or responses. Often marketing research or customer insight teams generate surveys and solicit customer feedback about pricing. The (self-reported) opinions invariably show that customers think firm's prices are too high. In this book I recommend modelling not what a customer says but what a customer does. That's why in terms of (an existing product) price, actual transactions and actual choices (from a transactional database) in an economic environment are advocated rather than a survey.

5 Because retail operates on thin margins this book provides targeted marketing and loyalty design and analytics.

A large part of this book, again from a marketing orientation, will be on targeting and loyalty analytics. Targeting is about using predictive models to ascertain which customers will respond or purchase, when they will respond or purchase, or how much they will buy. Loyalty analytics is about degrees of customer satisfaction, competitive density and convenience of products and the path to purchase.

Again, there are three general uses of data and analytics. The lowest type (which is probably a necessary but not sufficient step) is *descriptive*. This step tends to use past or historical data and really summarizes what happened. The next type is *predictive*. It is in this stage that most of this book will dwell. This is the statistical analytic process of estimating what causes what. It is not necessarily about forecasting the future (which requires forecasting the independent variables forward into time) but is about estimating a (customer) event. That is, if price decreases, what impact will that have on individual customers in terms of purchasing more or purchasing sooner. The last step is prescriptive. This ultimate use of data and analytics strives to maximize (in a systemic way) some general metric, typically net margin, profit or satisfaction.

6 Because retail uses multi-touch points, channels or vehicles, this book is channel agnostic and shows analytic techniques to maximize channel and vehicle use.

By channel I mean online vs. offline (in store) and by vehicle I mean targeted vehicles: typically, direct mail, e-mail, SMS. (Whilst analytics has a place in mass media, I will barely deal with the topic in this book.) Knowing which channel or vehicle different customer segments prefer is critical. Sending direct mail catalogues to those that believe 'Print is dead!' is a waste of money. Sending e-mails to those that are tech wary creates e-mail fatigue and is as useless.

While we will model the contribution of marcomm on sales or units for example, the most interesting and strategic aspect is a technique called simultaneous equations. This is rather advanced but can quantify for example what impact an e-mail has on online sales vs. offline sales. We will return to this later.

Retail culture and corporate agility

In retail, merchandizers rule the world. They are supply- and logistics-oriented and have a strong financial bent. That is, they are designed to be antagonistic to marketing. Marketing is demand-oriented and key metrics are customer-focussed. In most large retail organizations, marketing reports to merchandizing. Marketing is always suspect, held in scorn and at best tolerated. Marketing's knowledge of customer behaviour is often seen as irrelevant. What marketing needs to do is provide analytics that will drive the business and make merchandizers listen. Because all business emotions come from either fear or greed, marketing analytics can decrease the chance of making a mistake and can pull strategic levers to maximize net margin. Each of these will cause merchandizers (as well as finance, operations, real estate, etc) to pay attention.

To be agile in a retail corporation, focus must be on metrics (same store sales) that drive the business. Because most retail organizations output a lot of data, it's easy to major on the minor things. For example, focussing on salvaging the current quarter by offering deeper discounts to make purchases happen now, at the expense of the next quarter. Also, focussing on very engaged customers (via RFM) but not learning what causes such engagement, or why lower valued customers are not engaged (maybe they are sensitive to price, prefer a different channel or need a different market basket bundle). The renowned Peter Drucker said the only three metrics that matter are increasing revenue and increasing satisfactions and decreasing expenses. And of course he's right. Do politics come into play? Of course, but if attention is on what drives the business, everything else falls into place.

Conclusion

Retail is an important and exciting place to work. The industry needs and profits from analytics more than most. As such, analysts need to understand and treat retail as unique, learn and apply particular tools and techniques in a particular way, to solve the specialized problems of retail.

Checklist

You'll be the smartest person in the room if you:

- [ ] Acknowledge that retail is a major industry full of a variety of unique opportunities and challenges.

- [ ] Point out that because retail has specific and unique problems, analytics needs to have specific and unique solutions.

RETAIL

Data uniqueness

Which CRM systems are used?

CRM (customer relationship management) has been around for decades. It is typically a customer service, marketing or sales function. In retail it tends to be geared to marketing. The idea is that marketing communications (marcomm) provides customers with the right offer at the right time via the right channel recommending the right product, in such a way that the customer feels the retailer really KNOWS them. This establishes a relationship, indeed, pushes a retailer toward providing nearly monopoly product, price, promotion and place.

In order to keep a pulse on the business most retailers have some business intelligence (BI) functions. These usually include tools like Tableau, Business Objects, Crystal or Brio reporting or even dumping from a database into Excel. The idea is to display trends and KPIs in some dashboard format, to let decision-makers know how the business is doing. This is all descriptive data.

Store, customer and marcomm analysis is the general framework. Each of these dimensions has a particular relevance to retail.

Store analysis is about size, growth and demographics of the trade area, differences in sales per square foot applied to store type (eg stand-alone, in a shopping mall, part of an anchor), competitive density, customer's distance/convenience to each store. Retailers are always opening and closing stores. Many of these KPIs are done by direct marketing area (DMA) to take into account general demographics, lifestyle, and other factors.

Customer analysis looks at KPIs involving amount of sales, time between transactions, share of product categories bought, price sensitivity, etc. Bundling product categories is a big part of customer analysis. This is entirely behavioural and the idea is to understand how customers behave and react in terms of transactions and marcomm.

Marcomm analysis focusses on issues such as channel and vehicle, offers sent and messages. There is an ROI in terms of cost, for example of direct mail and purchase results.

Sources of retail data

One reason to focus on the retail industry is due to the enormous amount, complexity and variety of data retail generates. There are many sources and dimensions that, if merged together, form a very interesting picture of customer behaviour.

POS is primary

Of course it starts with the point of sale (POS) system. This is the transactional and redemption database. This is the ultimate source of customer behaviour. Data that is typically used from this system is at a customer level: amount spent, what was purchased, when it was purchased, what tender type, what coupon used and what discount applied. Using this data, we often calculate discount percentage, price sensitivity, channel preference, share of product, time between visits, and seasonality.

Coupon redemption data

As just alluded to above, coupon redemption data is key to retail customers. This usually includes what marketing sends to each customer (via direct mail, e-mail and SMS) as well as merchandizer's mark-down prices, generating newspaper copy, free-standing offers, etc. A large part of retail analytics is around marketing communications (marcomm) and targeting and price sensitivity (elasticity modelling) and channel/vehicle preference.

Marcomm responses

To further emphasize the above, marcomm responses are very important to retail marketers. This needs to be more than mere descriptive data via BI. This analysis needs to be at the predictive level and if possible at the prescriptive level.

Most retailers invest a very large amount of money in marcomm. Understanding which customers are sensitive to the type and amount of discount, over what channel and with what vehicle is everything. For e-mails, opens and clicks and the click-through rate are standard metrics. Also note that SMS is increasing penetration and a large part of marketing strategy is about how to make better use of SMS.

Certainly social media is now a big part of what retailers track and invest in. Social media has made possible inbound marketing rather than only traditional outbound marketing. The added dimension of blogs and sentiment mentions give a different colour to typical marketing/marcomm strategies. A new and very powerful analytic project is about attribution modelling, eg how much weight should be given to positive mentions from the social sphere?

Overlay data

A valuable source for analytics is often overlay data. This is typically provided from another source that includes external variables. This can be demographics (including age, education, gender, size of household) and it can be life stage/lifestyle data. Lifestyle is usually about different interests (eg sky-diving, hobbies, crafts, race cars, jogging) and/or attitudes about the firm and its competitors such as satisfaction, loyalty, advertising awareness. Often valuable are data elements such as uses of blogs and newspapers, TV shows and magazines read, dependency upon word of mouth or positive or negative mentions in a forum. In general, demographics are not of much help in analytics, only in fleshing out certain aspects of analytics (eg after segmentation is done on behavioural variables, demographics help explain fuller profiles).

It is probably obvious that all of the above is meant to give insight and understanding into customer behaviour. When this and other data are used, for example, in segmentation, each segment (sub-market) ought to be uniquely differentiated in terms of motivating and sensitivities. Even data like clickstream, call-centre transcripts or social media preferences give a clue to what marketers (and others) have always wanted: a 360-degree view of customer behaviour. Also, marketing research is an important data source here, especially in terms of the above attitudes and interests and uses of the brand.

Required spiel on Big Data

Big Data (yes, you have to capitalize it!) is everywhere. You can't get away from it. It's in every post and every update and every blog and every article and every book and every résumé and every college class anywhere you look. It's inescapable. So now it's time to add to the fray.

What is Big Data?

No one knows. I'll provide a working definition here but it will evolve over the years.

First, Big Data is BIG

By 'Big' I mean many, many rows and many, many columns. Note that there is no magic threshold that suddenly puts us in the 'We are now in the Big Data range!' It's relative.

This brings us to the second and third dimension of what is Big Data: complexity.

Second, Big Data is potential multiple sources merged together

The dimension of Big Data came about because of the proliferation of multiple sources of data, both traditional and non-traditional.

So we have traditional data. This means transactions from activities such as POS and marcomm responses. This is what we've had for decades. We also created our own data, things like time between purchases, discount rate, seasonality, and click-through rate.

The next step was to add overlay data and marketing research data. This was third-party demographics and/or lifestyle data merged to the customer file. Marketing research responses could be merged to the customer file to provide things like satisfaction, awareness or competitive density.

Then came the first wave of different data: web logs. This was different and the first taste of Big Data. It is another channel. Merging it with customer data is a whole other process.

Now there is non-traditional data. I'm talking about merging social or digital data to individual customers. This is a whole new kind of technology or platform issue. But there are several companies who've developed technologies to scrape off the customer's ID – e-mail, link, handle, tag, etc – and merge with other data sources. This is key! This is clearly a very different kind of data but it shows us number of friends/connections, blog/post activity, sentiment, touch points, site visits and so on.

Third, Big Data is potential multiple structures merged together

Big Data has an element of degrees of structure. I'm talking about the very common structured data, through semi-structured and all the way to unstructured data. Structured data is the traditional codes that are expected by type and length – it is uniform. Unstructured data is everything but that. It can include text-mining from, say, call records and free-form comments; it can also include video, audio and graphics. Big Data gets us to structure this unstructured data.

Fourth, Big Data is analytically and strategically valuable

Just to be obvious: data that is not valuable can barely be called data. It can be called clutter or noise or trash. But it's true that what is trash to me might be gold to you. Take clickstream data. That URL has a lot in it. To the analyst, what is typically of value is the page the visitor came from and is going to, how long they were there, or what they clicked on. Telling me what web browser they used or whether it's an active server page or the time to load the wire frame (all probably critically important to some geek somewhere) is of little to no value to the analyst. So Big Data can generate a lot of stuff but there has to be a (eg text-mining) technique/technology to put it in a form that can be consumed. That's what makes it valuable – not the quantity but the quality.

Is it important?

Probably. As alluded to above, what multiple data sources can provide to the marketer is insight into consumer behaviour. It's important to the extent that it provides more touch points of the shopping and purchasing process. To know that one segment always looks at word-of-mouth opinions and blogs for the product in question is very important. To know that another segment reads reviews and puts a lot of attention on negative sentiment can be invaluable for marketing strategy (and PR).

Just as 20 years ago clickstream data provided another view of shopping and purchasing, Big Data adds layers of complexity. Because consumer behaviour is complex, added granularity is a benefit. But beware of 'majoring on the minors' or paralysis of analysis. Aim at action.

What does it mean for analytics? For strategy?

There needs to be a theory: THIS causes THAT. An insight has to be new and provide an explanation of causality and of a type that can be acted upon. Otherwise (no matter how BIG it is) it is meaningless. So the only value of Big Data is that it gives us a glimpse into the consumer's mindset, it shows us their 'path to purchase'.

For analytics this means a realm of attribution modelling that places weight on each touch point, by behavioural segment. Strategically, from a portfolio point of view, it tells us that this touch point is of value to shoppers/purchasers and this one is NOT. Therefore, attention needs to be paid to those touch points (eg pages, sites, networks, groups, communities, stores, blogs, influencers) that are important to consumers. The biggest difference that Big Data gives us is that now we have more things to look at, more complexity, and this cannot be ignored. To pretend consumers do not travel down that path is to be foolishly simplistic. For example, when a 3-dimensional globe is forced into a 2-dimensional (from a sphere to a wall) space, Greenland looks to be the size of Africa. The over-simplification created distortion. Same is true of consumer behaviour. The tip of the iceberg that we see is motivated by many unseen, below the surface, causes.

Why is it important?

Big Data is not going to go away. We will assimilate it. We will add its technological uniqueness to our own. We will be better for it.

The new data does not require new analytic techniques. The new data does not require new marketing strategies. Marketing is still marketing and understanding and incenting and changing consumer behaviour is still what marketers do. Now – as always – size does matter, and we have more. Enjoy!

Surviving the Big Data panic

How many times have you heard the following:

'New data – different data – Big Data!'

'We have a different data source. Throw out all we know about analytics and consumer behaviour and marketing strategy and start from scratch.'

'There are new data sources! Obviously the old ways need to be eliminated and we desperately need to design new algorithms and new strategies.'

Sound familiar? How many articles and books and blogs and forums and posts and seminars and e-mails announcing digital and non-traditional and Big Data have you seen? Every day! How many meetings have you attended where everyone shook their heads in worry? No one knows how to deal with these new sources of (unstructured) data. Divert all attention, stop everything now, because there are additional sources of consumer behaviour.

OK, take a deep breath. I'll make a few confessions and the first one is that I've been around nearly (gulp!) thirty years doing marketing analytics.

There have always been waves of data and it will continue. The 1970s introduced relational databases, storing data in hierarchical formats. Then in the 1980s came the emergence of business intelligence. That's when I started, doing analytics when we first merged POS with marcomm responses. This is small data. We thought recency, frequency, monetary (RFM) was very analytic! I saw the first panic then. People reached for things like the Taguchi method, which was about measuring inanimate objects from the manufacturing industry! It was misguided and inappropriate but it looked and sounded very trendy. New data sources required a new approach. Then we tested it in the field and it provided nothing but confusion.

The 1990s saw the introduction of the world wide web and the internet. Medium data. Clickstream data arrives, a new source of consumer behaviour. Of course we thought we needed a new algorithm and new strategies. Somehow we forgot it is still marketing, it is still consumer behaviour. Neural networks became vogue, and then chaos theory, and for the next 10 years I heard all about devices geared more for mystics than insights. Enter SAS with Enterprise Minor! Fortunately, David Shepherd (of the Direct Marketing Association) put a bounty on his website for any proof that neural networks etc outperformed traditional econometrics in the field. No one ever took that bounty.

The above is not to say that digital data IS NOT very different to traditional data. I LOVE clickstream data that shows just what page a consumer views, for how long and in what order. That is an amazing tracking of consumer behaviour. And the new social media is bringing about a paradigm shift from outbound marketing to inbound marketing. The same can be said for telematics or sensor data, text, time and location data, or RFID. They're different kinds of data but why would they require new statistical techniques? Are they not still about quantifying causality?

Consumers are still behaving, shopping, choosing and buying, aren't they? I advocate a practical application of traditional techniques applied to different kinds of (non-traditional and otherwise) data.

I'm not against new algorithms when needed. I typically do not think they are needed. I am also philosophically opposed to much of the conceptions that seem to be behind these new techniques, in that they try to remove the analyst from the analysis. (Maybe I'm old-fashioned.) The global chief strategy officer of a large prominent agency told me that the things I knew and the things I believed in are no longer valid. (He has a new job now, with a much, much smaller agency.)

Additional, different data does at least one good thing: it gives us new and deeper insights into consumer behaviour. For marketing analysts that is always a good idea.

Additional complexity, as appropriate, is the right dimension to pursue. Over-simplification is wrong. Thus, added dimensions of complexity is a valuable input.

We do not need to search for exotic algorithms or knee-jerk into wildly different strategies. We need to embrace the layers of information we have about consumer behaviour and take them all into account. We have analytic techniques (and have had for decades) for doing that very thing: simultaneous equations, structural equations, and vector autoregression for example. Yes, these are more complex and that is where our attention should be: learning to perfect modelling that incorporates explaining additional complexity in consumer behaviour. After all, marketing is, and has always been about, understanding and incenting and changing consumer behaviour. That will be no different when the next wave of data hits.

Big Data analytics

One point I'd like to clear up: Big Data and analytics. It's easy to get lost in the techno-jargon and noise around Big Data. In my simplistic view, let's say an analysis has these phases: 1) define the problem; 2) collect data; 3) apply algorithm; and 4) implement/output solution.

Has Big Data changed the first phase? No, probably not. The problem is still the same. Let's say marketers are trying to send communications to customers and get them to buy. Phase 1 is the same whether Big Data is included or used or accessible or not. Phase 2 does require some of the Big Data tools and processes and techniques (map reduce/Hadoop). Even some of the text-mining will require the ability to turn unstructured data into structured data, so some natural language programming is necessary. Now, for our purposes does Big Data require different algorithms? As mentioned above, my view it that (so far) it DOES NOT. Ordinary regression will work, logistic regression will answer many questions, segmentation is the right approach.

For Phase 4 I would suggest there are some Big Data tools to implement in real time. So in my contrived example of an analytics solution to a business problem, the framing of the questions and the analytics itself can be done independently of Big Data technology and processes. I'm trying to draw a line here that says the technology is on one side and the questions and analysis are on the other side. Disagree if you like.

Conclusion

Retail has a lot of data and most of this data can be tied directly to consumer behaviour. This is a very good thing. One of the best things about the retail industry is that it has its ear close to what the consumer says and it can see (sometimes immediately) what the consumer wants and what works. Be grateful for this glut of data. It provides answers; you just have to know the questions and how to answer them.

Checklist

You'll be the smartest person in the room if you:

☐ Are grateful for the depth and breadth of typical data in retail. Retail industries have a lot of data from a wide variety of sources and this makes our analytic job more robust.

☐ Advocate the merging of a wide variety of retail data from as many sources as feasible: point-of-sale system, responses from the e-mail service provider, overlay data, marketing research, etc.

☐ Don't panic and lose focus on Big Data. Remember, it is just another source of data (just as clickstream data was a new source in the mid-1990s).

INTERLUDE

Now that we've got through the preliminaries (overview of statistics, data and the retail industry) it's time to focus on what this book is really trying to do: give marketers insights into customer behaviour that will drive the business. Each chapter will start with a general marketing question and then provide an analytic answer to that question. Then a business case will detail the use and output involved in using marketing science to answer the marketing strategy question.

This means that, after the Chapter 2 introduction to regression and factor analysis, reading the book in order isn't necessary. Generally, I'd suggest flipping through to find the marketing problem you're dealing with and that chapter will give you an analytic answer to that problem. This means that each chapter is nearly stand-alone.

However, it is also true that the chapters on dependent variable techniques (eg regression modelling) are organized in increasing complexity: ordinary regression, logistic regression and Poisson regression, survival modelling and simultaneous equations. So if your marketing problem involved, say, multiple stages and the answer is simultaneous equations, while it is generally designed to 'stand alone', you might want to review ordinary regression.

UNDERSTANDING AND ESTIMATING DEMAND

MARKETING QUESTION

How can I estimate demand? What things impact demand?

ANALYTIC SOLUTION

Ordinary regression

Introduction

So our first question is a basic and very important one: how do you estimate demand? By 'demand' is typically meant (especially in retail circles) units or quantity. That is, the number of total items purchased. This is not the number of transactions or amount of net revenue but the count of items in the basket. Two packs of batteries count as two units even if they are only one stock-keeping unit (SKU).

Is there an issue in defining the dependent variable as units when one unit can include a set of AA batteries as well as a giant screen TV? No, not really. Regression is always 'on average' and a unit is a unit, on average. However the merchandizers construct the product hierarchy in defining units is what we'll use. Besides, what else can we do? Remember, a simplifying assumption always puts us on the right path.

(It is possible of course to add deeper granularity by making a demand model not just total units but units of a particular product category, eg consumer electronics or newborn/infant/toddler products. That is, do a separate demand model for each major product category. I would say this is a Phase 2 project, after the proof-of-concept of total demand is understood and socialized.)

So demand is fundamental to the business. How many units are we selling? Obviously the number of units we sell at each price is what gives us total revenue which at the end of the day is really the name of the game. Microeconomics is all about the interplay between units and price. This is what Alfred Marshall gave us: those wonderful supply and demand graphs that detail the inverse relationship between price and quantity. He displayed both the consumption side (consumer behaviour) and the production side (firm behaviour). Most of this book will be about the demand side as much of analytics will be from a marketing point of view and the frame of interest is consumer behaviour.

Quick note: units can be measured as counts, and to the extent that there are few of them or the distribution is skewed (non-normal) Poisson regression should be used rather than ordinary regression (see Chapter 15 on Poisson regression). This chapter will assume normality and advocate ordinary regression.

Business objective

So, what is the business objective? In simple terms it is to quantify causality. That is, generate a hypothesis that says this causes that. Price causes demand. Advertising causes demand. Seasonality causes demand.

All models should have an independent variable that can be a 'lever' for a marketer to pull to affect the output, in this case, demand. Remember that demand consists of units, which economists call quantity. So if price is an independent variable (ie significant), then the strategy can be to pull the price lever in order to change the quantity demanded. If advertising is an independent variable the strategy can be to change advertising so that will change demand. While there will be some other variable(s) that the marketer has no control over (seasonality, for example) if the model is entirely comprised of variables that the marketer cannot change then there will be no strategic impact and it is of limited use. Marketing is about 'action-ability'.

So the user of the model wants two things: an estimate of demand and a way to change the estimate. Note that for now we are not talking about forecasting per se. Forecasting is about predicting the future amount of demand, typically by a future prediction of the independent variables. Later we will deal with that very topic. So note that in this chapter estimating is not forecasting. We are predicting demand based on independent variables, not forecasting the independent variables into a future time period in order to predict what demand will be in the future.

Using ordinary regression to estimate demand

A primer on ordinary regression

OK, let's start at square one: ordinary regression. Ordinary regression is a dependent variable technique. This means there is one equation and that one equation has an output variable. That output variable is hypothesized to DEPEND on one or more independent variables. Remember back in algebra:

$$Y = mX + B$$

That is the equation of a straight line. Y, in this case the output variable, exactly depends on an intercept (B) and an average slope (m) and an independent variable (X). This is analogous to simple ordinary regression. That equation is typically written as:

$$Y = a + BX + e$$

where Y is again the output variable that depends on an intercept (a constant, a) and an average slope B and an independent variable. (As to why mathematicians call the intercept B and statisticians call the intercept a, and why mathematicians call the slope parameter m and statisticians call it B – I don't know. I suspect it has something to do with the deep-rooted hatred they have for each other, but I could be wrong.)

The big difference is that regression is statistical and not mathematical. Regression estimates a stochastic process. That means that Y does not exactly depend on an intercept and an average slope and the various independent variable(s). Y also depends, on average, on the random variation of e, an unseen, unmeasured fluctuation. In statistics, the dependent variable depends, on average, on the fixed parameters, a and B, and the independent variable(s).

Properties of estimators

The logic of ordinary regression is to fit parameters (the intercept/constant and the one or more (slope) coefficients on each independent variable) in such a way as to maximize some criteria. It happens (in terms of ordinary least squares, OLS) that the criterion is to 'minimize the sum of the squared errors'. Thus the parameters are fitted in order to meet the criteria, given the variance in the dependent and the independent variable(s). That is, OLS finds the line that 'fits best', defined as minimizing the sum of the squared errors. (The calculus involved in this minimization is not advanced and can be found in nearly any introductory econometrics textbook.)

Thus these estimators are chosen with some care, in order to meet some criteria. That is, good estimators have particular properties. A few of the common/important ones are detailed below.

Unbiasedness

Unbiasedness uses inductive reasoning and is a bit theoretical. The idea is that a large number of (repeated) samples are taken wherein the independent variables are constant but new values of the dependent variable are seen by having different values of the error term. If an ordinary regression is estimated on each sample, the values of the beta coefficient would change. If the values of the beta coefficient were plotted they would (by assumption) track a normal distribution. The mean of the normal distribution of the beta coefficient sampling distribution would be the true (population) parameter value. Note that the difference in the sample coefficient and population coefficient is the amount of bias.

Now, some econometricians live and die by unbiasedness and some do not. I myself do not. I have found that the more academic of us tend to be very interested in unbiasedness and the more applications-oriented of us tend not to care much for it. The reason why I do not put a lot of stock in unbiasedness is because we typically have (in the real world) only ONE sample. We do not have a large number of samples. We never know whether our sample is a 'good' one or a 'bad' one (or even an 'average' one) but hope that on average it will work. That is, we can do very little about it. While the idea is important in terms of supporting/defending practical assumptions, most of the practical marketing scientists take cold comfort in unbiasedness.

Efficiency

The idea of efficiency is simple. Out of all the unbiased estimators, the efficient one is that which has the smallest variance.

Consistency

The above (unbiasedness and consistency) are small sample properties. Consistency is asymptotic, that is, a large sample property. Consistency is the property that as n increases to infinity, the (on average) estimate on beta collapses onto the true population parameter.

A note on time series data: autocorrelation

For this first demand model, we will use time series data. That is, each row is a period of time, in this case a week. It'll look like Table 5.1. More or less other data can be added.

TABLE 5.1   Time series data

week	units	net price	# trans	avg disc	gross price	gross rev	# dms	# ems	# sms
4/1/2015	1,055,100	45.25	23,446	11.4%	50.41	53,186,008	7,034	28,516	9,592
11/1/2015	1,076,100	44.60	23,911	11.6%	49.77	53,561,371	7,174	29,084	9,783
18/1/2015	1,097,500	44.00	24,399	12.8%	49.63	54,471,120	7,317	29,662	9,977
25/1/2015	1,119,600	43.50	24,800	12.7%	49.02	54,887,830	7,464	30,259	10,178
1/2/2015	1,141,600	42.00	25,399	13.7%	47.75	54,515,966	7,611	30,854	10,378
8/2/2015	1,164,900	42.00	25,995	14.0%	47.88	55,775,412	7,766	31,484	10,590
15/2/2015	1,188,200	41.30	26,300	14.7%	47.37	56,286,341	7,921	32,114	10,802
22/2/2015	1,211,700	41.00	26,965	16.0%	47.56	57,628,452	8,078	32,749	11,015

Time series data is very common in econometrics, but has an inherent characteristic which violates one of the key assumptions: no serial correlation. This is the assumption that error terms are not correlated with each other. Unfortunately, in time series data serial (auto) correlation is endemic; the only question is 'To what extent?' What we'll mostly deal with is called 1st-order autocorrelation and it is the correlation between each error and the (one period) lagged error. That is, the error term on the first week is correlated with the error term on the second week, the error term on the second week is correlated with the error term on the third week, and so on. So 1st-order correlation is the correlation between the error terms and the lagged error term. This can be shown by the equation:

$$e_t = \rho e_{t-1} + v_t \text{ where}$$
$$e_t = \text{error term at time t}$$
$$\rho = \text{correlation and}$$
$$v_t = \text{random error}$$

Consequences of violation

Even though the parameter estimates are unbiased (that is, on average the parameter estimates are unbiased – any one sample could be way too high or way too low and they merely cancel each other out), there are two disastrous consequences of autocorrelation. This is why it must be diagnosed and corrected.

The first is a large variance in the error term. This means that the parameter estimates (for the coefficients of the independent variables) are inefficient.

The second is that the standard error of the parameter estimates are biased and they are (typically) biased downward. That is, t-ratios $(\beta/_{se}\beta)$ will look better (be higher) than they really are and you may accept an independent variable as significant when it really is not. This means R^2 can also be inflated. Again, this is why you must test and correct for autocorrelation.

Detection

The most common way to detect (1st-order AR(1) autocorrelation) is with the Durbin–Watson statistic. (Other tests exist for other AR processes, eg the Durbin-h test.) The DW stat is an output of all real analytic packages, eg SAS, SPSS. Generally speaking, the closer this is to 2.0 the less chance there is that damaging autocorrelation exists in the data-set. (There is an 'indeterminate zone' endemic with the DW stat and any econometric text can give the details.) This test needs to be run before and after 'correction' so now we'll get to the correction.

Correction

The general correction is fairly straightforward. What's needed is an estimate of the correlation between lagged error terms. Then that estimate is used in a 'quasi-differencing' process to 'correct' autocorrelation. This is accomplished through the Cochran–Orcutt procedure and should be an option for every analytic software package available.

The quasi-differencing procedure is:

1 Apply a lag function on both dependent and independent variables.
2 Multiply these variables by the estimated correlation.
3 'Difference' the data, that is new $Y = Y_t - \rho Y_{t-1}$ etc.
4 Run ordinary regression on the new data.
5 Test again the DW stat. If it's closer to 2.0 you have decreased autocorrelation.

Dummy variables

Binary variables are those that take on only two values: 0 or 1. They are usually called dummy variables. They are important as independent variables because they can test for an effect. Often they are to score qualitative ideas like married or not, male or not, African–American or not, Q1 or not.

Dummy variables are used because nominal variables are non-quantitative. Let's say we believe the season or quarter is important – and it typically is. So we have a variable called 'quarter' with four values: 1 for Q1, 2 for Q2, 3 for Q3 and 4 for Q4. This coefficient would show an average impact taking quarters into account. We do not want an average quarterly impact; we want to know how one individual quarter shifts the value of the dependent variable compared to another quarter. For this there needs to be a variable for Q1 that takes on the value of 1 when the time period is IN Q1 and 0 otherwise. There also needs to be a variable called Q2 that takes on the value of 1 when the time period is IN Q1 and 0 otherwise. In this way the specific impact of each quarter can be measured and taken into account which is far more accurate than one variable taking on an average of all quarters.

However, when using dummy variables you must take care to avoid the 'dummy trap'. (This is probably why they are called dummy variables.) For example, say you were doing a quarterly model and used all four variables Q1, Q2, Q3 and Q4, each with a 0 or 1 value. Note that if you sum the system of variables called quarter every time period would equal 1 and there would be no variance. The regression equation could not compute. You must use LESS than the number of dummy variables. It does not matter which quarter you drop but you must drop (at least) one quarter. Say you drop Q1 and keep Q2 and Q3 and Q4. The interpretation of the coefficients now changes. They are now all compared to the variable dropped, in this case, to Q1. If the coefficient on Q2 is 150, the interpretation is 'whenever the time period is IN Q2 the dependent variable increases by 150 MORE THAN COMPARED TO Q1'. See?

Business case

On to the business case. First a little set-up. Say we have an analyst, Scott who just switched jobs. He was an analytic manager for a PC manufacturing firm and is now director of CRM and database marketing at a general retailing firm. He has a staff of about seven people. This includes programmers as well as modellers. Mark is the senior modeller of the group and has been there many years. The group's main objectives are targeted list pulls for direct mail, e-mail and SMS. They do not do reporting. They often help with campaign test cell designs, give guidance on general forecasting, discount analysis, sometimes even about trade area analysis. Generally, this group is in the marketing organization but as mentioned has light 'consulting' duties with merchandizing, finance, real estate and operations.

So one of Scott's first projects was to design a demand model. His boss Becky (VP of customer insights) met with him and described the need.

'I brought you in Scott based on several projects you described at your last job. I was particularly interested in demand. Forecasting, elasticity, etc. What do you need to give us insights into demand?'

'Well,' Scott said, 'I'll get my gang together and formulate the problem and collect data and go down the road.'

'I see. How long do you think it'll take?'

'We can probably estimate a general model in a few weeks and then we'll give the output and talk about next steps. Does this need to be by product category, by segment, by region, etc?'

'Probably. Eventually. Let's take it one step at a time.'

Scott called his team together and they met in the conference room.

'OK,' Scott said. 'The issue is modelling demand. By demand I mean quantity. Units.'

'Well,' one of the analysts suggested, 'we have units easily enough from our POS system. Is this just collecting weekly units and graphing trends? We already have a report that does that.'

Scott nodded. 'Yes, thanks, I know. That is descriptive only. That tells us nothing except a general trend. It does not tell us WHY units are moving up or down, WHY a spike or dip occurred. It does not give us a way to increase units. It does not give us a business case on how to make our spending more efficient. That is, it gives us no insights, no strategy.'

The analyst slunk down in his chair.

'Yes,' another analyst said. 'It's a regression problem, right? We're trying to see what independent variables explain the movement in the dependent variable. In this case units.'

'Right, I think so,' Scott said. 'We start with what question are we trying to answer.'

'What explains the movement in units?'

'Right.'

'We've done some trending and correlations earlier,' mentioned the first analyst. 'We have a strong seasonal pattern, as do most retailers. So we know seasonality is a cause.'

'I'm sure of it,' Scott said. The analyst smiled. 'But how does that help us?'

'Well, we want to know what causes movement in units and seasonality causes movement in units.'

'Right. But what do we do with that? What levers does that give us to pull?'

They all looked at him.

'What strategic advantage does knowing seasonality give us? Not much. Seasonality, as a pattern, is not really in our control. What we need is a demand model that explains the movement in units by collecting variables that are, and are not, in our control.'

'Like what?'

'Like the marketing mix: product, price, promotion and place. Are customers sensitive to a change in price, for example? Would that affect demand?'

'Yes, sure.'

'What about marketing communications? Does sending out catalogues or e-mails or advertising promotions or product offers affect demand?'

'They better.'

'Right. Those are direct marketing, but also mass media, advertising, should move the needle on units.'

'Which is why we spend millions of dollars on TV.'

Scott nodded. 'So, framing the question is the start. Becky's question is not just about what moves demand. Her real question is what moves demand that she has control over. If we would just use seasonality – which we know to be a factor – and consumer confidence, tastes and preferences, competitive density, we would explain a large part of the movement of demand. But that would not give Becky any lever to pull – and that is really her question.'

The group smiled and nodded. Scott thought now was a good time for a break. Instead he went back to his office and wrote data requirements.

The next day his team met in his office and looked over what he had written on his white board.

'Each row is a week, a time series model,' Scott said.

'There's a lot of data there. Advertising spend, different marcomm, different price points, different events, seasonality, and more.'

'Yes, but we have a lot of observations so degrees of freedom will not be an issue.'

'We'll probably do it with stepwise,' the analyst said, 'which will make it go faster.'

'Oh,' Scott stopped. 'Here's a rule: no one on my team is allowed ever to use stepwise or any other automated variable selection process.'

They all looked at him. Clearly he had crossed a line.

'The idea is that stepwise and other automated selection processes eliminate the brain from the analyst,' Scott said. 'It tries to put us out of a job by suggesting what we do is just a matter of mathematics. Automated selection maximizes the F-test, chi-square, etc, to choose the "best" independent variables.'

'Yes, and isn't that what we want to do?'

'Maybe not,' Scott said. 'I mean, there's more to analytics than just choosing independent variables that maximize the chi-square test. It's sometimes preferable to have a variable in the model that does not maximize some test metric, or maybe even if the variable is insignificant. For instance, what if the t-ratio on price was 1.55. To have 95 per cent confidence the t-ratio should be 1.96. But there may be times when you'll trade some significance for the insight that keeping the variable in the model offers. In this example I would believe that price is a driver of demand even if the sample we have suggests that price is not 95 per cent significant.'

'I see. No stepwise. Use my brain.'

'Good. Your job as analyst is to put variables in the model that you believe generate the data we have, that is, you have a causality theory and put those variables in and test them. That's what modelling is all about.'

'So we collect this data and we're going to do ordinary regression, with units as the dependent variable?'

'Right. So this will be time series, you'll have to check and correct for serial correlation.'

'Using the Durbin–Watson test?'

'Yes, if it's an AR(1) process. Let's get back together at the end of the week and see what we have.'

The next week Scott's team came in with some first draft output. The overhead projector provided its usual technical difficulty but eventually it worked and displayed Table 5.2.

TABLE 5.2   Time series data: model output

VAR	COEFF	SE ERR	T-RATIO
net price	−2.06	1.57	−1.31
# dms	10.76	4.65	+2.31
# ems	−0.86	0.46	−1.88
# sms	5.66	2.67	+2.12
Q1	−23,506.32	11,503.23	−2.04
Q2	−5,509.65	1,500.50	−3.67
Q3	−503.65	250.65	−2.01
DW	1.22		
VAR	**COEFF**	**SE ERR**	**T-RATIO**
net price	−2.95	1.62	−1.82
# dms	11.76	5.13	+2.29
# ems	−0.96	0.49	−1.95
# sms	5.96	2.90	+2.05
Q1	−20,655.32	12,652.33	−1.63
Q2	−7,566.65	1,495.66	−5.06
Q3	−539.56	276.66	−1.95
DW	1.99		

'So this shows the first and final run of the model,' said the analyst. 'Note the DW went from 1.22 to 1.99, so we probably eliminated autocorrelation. Some of the estimates on the variables changed as well, especially the standard error.'

'Makes sense,' said Scott. 'Autocorrelation tends to bias downward the standard errors. I see net price is not at 95 per cent, but close enough. A t-ratio of 1.96 would be 95 per cent, so 1.82 is pretty good. And I absolutely believe that price should be significant in a demand model.'

'Agreed.'

'You're comparing all the quarters to Q4 and they are all negative, nice. Q1 is VERY negative.' Scott smiled at them and continued. 'I also like how it gives marketers a marcomm lever. Look at direct mail, a coefficient of 11.76 means for every thousand DMs sent units on average increase by 11,760. Outstanding!'

'Yes, but look at e-mail. It's actually negative.'

'And virtually 95 per cent significant.'

'What will we tell them? Want me to delete it?'

Scott shot him a look. 'Definitely not. Let's think about what causality causes that.'

'It means the more e-mails we send out the less units we get, taking everything else into account.'

'Yes, that's the interpretation. What are you going to tell marketing? Want to tell Becky not to send out e-mails?'

They looked at each other. A couple shifted in their seats.

'Yes, we know there's the possibility of e-mail fatigue and we have talked before about sending out so many e-mails we just bother people.'

Scott shrugged. 'It's really about targeting anyway, right? Some of our customers probably appreciate e-mails, certainly those with a relevant call to action. But overall just blasting the phone book with e-mails does not work.'

'Right. It's because e-mails are free. Marketing thinks there is no cost to sending out a gazillion e-mails.'

'But they're not actually free, are they? There is a hardware/network cost and a creative cost and now we are seeing a loss of interest in our e-mails. So there is customer-relevance cost. We'll deal with this later, especially in a segmentation framework.'

'By the way the R^2 was over 84 per cent,' the analyst pointed out.

'What about adjusted R^2?' Scott asked.

'I have it here.' He fumbled though his stack of output. '82.6 per cent.'

'That's fine,' Scott said. 'We will always report adjusted R^2, not R^2.'

'But what's the difference?'

'R^2 cannot go down, if you add an independent variable – any independent variable. Adjusted R^2 will penalize the fit if the benefit of added explanatory power does not offset the cost of loss of degrees of freedom. That is, adjusted R^2 CAN go down.'

'Got it, thanks. I never knew that.'

'So let's set up a meeting and go over our preliminary results with Becky and marketing. Make sure to invite marketing strategy as well. And marketing communications.'

'All of them?'

'We're talking about demand here. All of them should be keenly interested in what causes demand. Oh, and tell them this is a lids-down meeting.'

They all looked at him.

Scott continued. 'Lids-down means no typing e-mails on their laptop or cellphone during the meeting. We need their attention.'

So Scott went home that night excited by the insights a demand model can bring. He was well aware it would drive them down a long road: elasticity, marcomm valuation, etc. But that was why he got the medium bucks.

Conclusion

Demand modelling is basic to marketing analytics. Understanding and quantifying major drivers of units are key components for marketers to use as levers to change the amount and velocity of units which give direct impact to revenue.

It is common to do regression on overall units, but better granularity and better strategy can result if the demand is at a lower level, eg a major category (such as consumer electronics, women's clothing). This becomes even more powerful if the category demand modelling is by (behavioural) segment.

Much of demand modelling is time series data and this requires dealing with serial correlation. SAS (and most other software packages) are ready-made to detect and correct this common violation of the assumption of 'no serial correlation'.

It's important to note that, even with time series modelling, there is not necessarily a 'forecast' involved. A forecast is a prediction (using a model) for a period in the future, typically involving predicting the independent variables into future time periods in order to produce a future dependent variable. This chapter is about a prediction (an estimate) of the dependent variable using a model. We will get to forecasting proper soon enough.

Checklist

You'll be the smartest person in the room if you:

- [ ] Remember that while ordinary regression is a major marketing analytic technique and, in terms of estimating demand is often the best choice, it comes with baggage and assumptions.

- [ ] Focus demand estimation on dealing with collinearity. Because collinearity can switch signs, including the sign-on price which is always hypothesized as negative, it must be detected and corrected.

- [ ] Require marketing insights. In order to generate marketing insights there must be marketing variables, eg marcomm (number of or spend on direct mail, e-mail, SMS), price, bundles offered, incentivizing channel.

- [ ] Make sure when using binary variables you avoid the 'dummy trap'.

- [ ] Never use stepwise procedures!

PRICE ELASTICITY AND DISCOUNTS

06

MARKETING QUESTION

How can I target discounts? Who needs a discount in order to maximize purchase probability? How much?

ANALYTIC SOLUTION

Elasticity modelling

Elasticity modelling is of utmost importance, especially in retail industries. Retail typically discounts too much (and they know it) but they have no real way to target or test or understand (quantitatively) just how to wean themselves off the drug. It is clear some customers do need a (deep) discount in order to maximize probability to purchase and it is also usually the case other customers (particularly for some product categories and/or at some times of the year) do NOT need a (deep) discount in order to purchase. It is the task of marketing analytics to understand and exploit this sensitivity to price.

The general approaches tend to be from marketing research, often in departments with names like 'shopper' or 'customer insights'. They often design primary research and, in terms of pricing, they basically ask their customers, 'Are our prices too high?' And do you know what the answer is? 'Yes! Your prices are too high!' That's what we call insights!? Now they'll add some bells and whistles and granularity and slide some sophistication in there but basically their customers say, 'We need a very deep discount in order to buy anything at all.' And they show this, even though it's self-reported and certainly self-serving.

Another common market research approach is the van Westendorp pricing analysis survey (PAS). This again is a self-reported survey-based approach. The unique thing about the PAS is that it essentially graphs two questions: at what price is the product too high to buy and at what price is the product too cheap to buy? The PAS posits the intersection of these lines is the 'optimal price'. As an econ man I believe the consumer's problem is 'How to maximize satisfaction by choosing products while operating under a limited budget'. I do not see how the intersection of those two lines addresses the consumer's problem.

The last typical approach is a conjoint analysis. Conjoint is powerful overall but in terms of giving pricing recommendation it fails from the same problems as all survey-based research: it is self-reported and it is not actual choices in a real economic environment. It is artificial. (For more on this, see Grigsby, 2015.)

That's why, for an existing product, if a database is available that tracks customer's actual purchases and responses to actual marketing communications offering actual changes in price, elasticity analysis is the only real solution.

Introduction to elasticity

Elasticity, as such, is an unfortunate term. It's a little awkward, cumbersome and not exactly even accurate. The right word is 'sensitivity.' The concept is a measure of how sensitive an output variable (typically units) is to a change in some input variable (and in this case that'll be price). That is, given a percentage change in price, what is the resultant percentage change in units?

We like the idea of elasticity because it is what mathematicians call a pure number: it is without dimension or scale. Whether units are measured in thousandths or tenths, whether price is in millions or one hundredths, the scale is irrelevant. This is because elasticity is a marginal function over an average function.

The term came from Alfred Marshall nearly 100 years ago. He was an English mathematician and he wrote a book, *Principles of Economics,* that went through many editions and made him famous. He was the one who gave to undergraduates those supply and demand graphs they love so well. He was the one who came up with the concept of elasticity.

There are two kinds of elasticity: elastic and inelastic, that is, sensitive and insensitive. When price changes by X per cent and units change by greater than X per cent, we say units are sensitive to price. When price changes by X per cent and units change by less than X per cent, we call this insensitive to price. Note that the relationship between units and price is always inverse, that is, negative. When price goes up units will go down. That is the only law in all of economics, the law of demand. So there is an inverse relationship between price and units just as there is an inverse relationship between mph and IQ. Because it is always calculated as negative we usually ignore the sign. That is, we always take the absolute value. If the elasticity is < 1.00 we call it inelastic and if it is > 1.00 we call it elastic.

(A quick note on demand modelling. This framework specifically assumes a horizontal supply curve meaning changing demand has no impact on the market-clearing price. This assumption seems fair, especially in the short term when most retail marketing happens. This also gets us out of the identity problem, which is accounted for with simultaneous equations.)

While price has an impact on units, the real magic of elasticity is the effect on total revenue. Note that total revenue = price * units. In an inelastic demand curve total revenue follows price. That means if you want to increase total revenue you must INCREASE price. In an elastic demand curve total revenue follows units. If you want to increase total revenue you must DECREASE price. By price I mean (and will always mean) NET price, that is, after discounts.

Note Figure 6.1 below. The top graph is the typical price–unit demand curve. It displays the inverse relationship as expected. Price is on the vertical axis and units on the horizontal axis. The bottom graph shows units and total revenue. Note that at the higher end of the units axis total

FIGURE 6.1   Relationship between price, units and total revenue

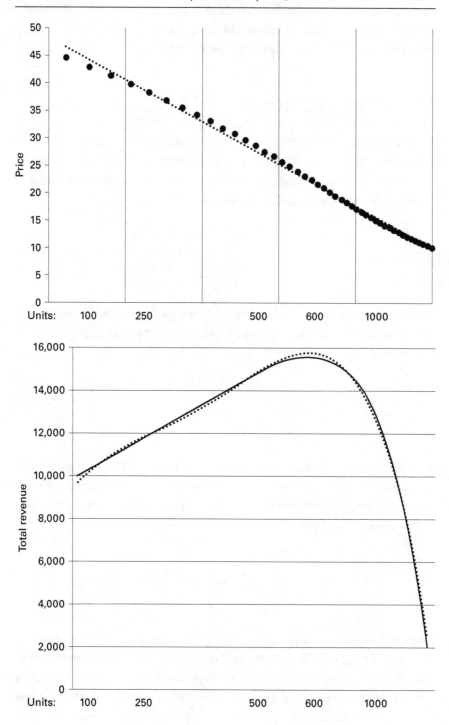

revenue can only increase if there is a price increase. That part of the demand curve is inelastic. The opposite is true at the lower end of units which have the higher end of prices. In order to increase total revenue price must be decreased. That is the elastic portion of the demand curve.

Modelling elasticity

To understand how modelling elasticity works, it's important to go from the mathematical to the statistical definition. When first exposed to elasticity the simple idea was demonstrated with 'point elasticity', that is, the elasticity between two points. Below, Q is quantity (units) and P is price:

$$\frac{\dfrac{(Q2 - Q1)}{Q1}}{\dfrac{(P2 - P1)}{P1}} \equiv$$

This is where we get the expression, 'Mind your Ps and Qs.' Anyway, after point elasticity we are next exposed to arc elasticity, that is, the elasticity of a larger part of the demand curve:

$$\frac{\dfrac{(Q2 - Q1)}{Q1}}{\dfrac{(P2 - P1)}{P1}} \equiv \frac{\dfrac{\Delta Q}{Q}}{\dfrac{\Delta P}{P}} \equiv$$

That is, the difference in the two points from quantity mathematically becomes the change in quantity and the difference in the two points from price mathematically becomes the change in price. This change in quantity over Q divided by change in price over P is the arc:

$$\frac{\dfrac{(Q2 - Q1)}{Q1}}{\dfrac{(P2 - P1)}{P1}} \equiv \frac{\dfrac{\Delta Q}{Q}}{\dfrac{\Delta P}{P}} \equiv \frac{dQ}{dP}\frac{\bar{P}}{\bar{Q}} \equiv$$

Now comes the fun part. Change in Q over change in P is the marginal function. That is, how Q changes as P changes shows an average slope of the whole (demand) function. This average slope in mathematics is called the derivative of Q with respect to P. So mathematically, elasticity is the marginal function over an average function, or the derivative of Q with respect to P multiplied by average P over average Q. Now comes the kicker:

$$\frac{dQ}{dP}\frac{\bar{P}}{\bar{Q}} \equiv Bprice \frac{\bar{P}}{\bar{Q}}$$

The average slope in mathematics is called the derivative. It is measured without error, all points on the function exactly equate to the function. In statistics the function is not measured without error, but includes a random error term, e. But the concept of average slope is in statistics; in ordinary regression it is called the coefficient. So the coefficient in statistics is analogous to the derivative in mathematics. So in a demand model where quantity is the dependent variable and price is the independent variable, to calculate elasticity requires multiplying the coefficient of price by average price over average quantity.

This elasticity calculation will always be negative, given that the price coefficient is negative (because of the inverse relationship between price and quantity). Therefore, by custom it is always reported as the absolute value, meaning that it is always reported as positive. If this calculation is < 1.00 it is on the inelastic portion of the demand curve and if it is > 1.00 it is on the elastic portion of the demand curve.

Just to ensure that the idea of elasticity as driving total revenue is clear, see Table 6.1. In the top portion is an example of inelasticity, 0.075. Note it is < 1.00. Price starts out at 10.00 and units start out at 1,000.00 and total revenue is therefore price * units = 10,000. Now increase price by 10%, so it goes from 10.00 to 11.00. Units go in the opposite direction, downward, by 0.75%, or from 1,000 to 993. Now total revenue is 10,918. That is, total revenue went up, price went up and units went down.

The converse is true in the bottom part of Table 6.1. This is the elastic portion of the demand curve at 1.25. Note that 1.25 > 1.00. We have the same starting positions of price and units and total revenue. Price is again increased by 10% from 10.00 to 11.00 but units (which still go down) decrease to 875 (1,000.00 * 0.875 (or 1.00–.125)) and total revenue goes down to 9,625. That is price went up. Remember, in order to increase total revenue in the elastic portion, price must go DOWN.

TABLE 6.1   Elasticity example

INELAST	0.075		increase price by	10.00%
p1	10.00	p2	11.00	10.00%
u1	1000.00	u2	993.00	−0.75%
tr1	10000.00	tr2	10918.00	9.20%
ELAST	**1.25**		**increase price by**	**10.00%**
p1	10.00	p2	11.00	10.00%
u1	1000.00	u2	875.00	−12.50%
tr1	10000.00	tr2	9625.00	−3.80%

A note about modelling elasticity in logs

It so happens that a marginal function over and average function is mathematically a logarithm function. Thus it's tempting to take the natural log of all variables (lnQ, lnP, etc) and run OLS. Then instead of calculating elasticity as the price coefficient multiplied by average price over average units, just read it off the (log model) beta coefficient only. While this is easier, (in my view) it also carries with it a heroic assumption: constant elasticity. That is, the units have the same response to any price change, small or large. I myself do not believe this.

It should also be pointed out that most economists believe demand is multiplicative. That is $Q = P*A*S$, where Q = quantity, P = price, A = advertising and S = seasonality. This model, while theoretically having good properties, is not linear regression. The model can be made linear by taking the log of all the variables. So, as is often the case, you must pick your poison. That is, there is both an art and a science to analytics. If you, as the analyst cannot stomach either multiplicative demand or constant elasticity, then you need to make clear you will not be using double log formulation.

Collinearity

One of the assumptions (it is not strictly speaking an assumption but a mathematical necessity) is 'no perfect collinearity in any of the independent variables'. If there is perfect collinearity – which essentially means one variable is some mathematical operation of another variable – the algorithm will not solve; it would be like dividing by zero. But the assumption is that there is no 'near perfect' collinearity. Of course that is a little arbitrary.

Collinearity is defined as one or more independent variables that are more correlated with each other than either of them is with the dependent variable. For example, if there are two independent variables in the model, damaging collinearity is if X_1 and X_2 are more correlated than X_1 and Y and/or X_2 and Y.

The result of having collinearity does not affect the parameter estimates; they remain unbiased. But the standard errors are too wide. This means when significance testing is calculated (parameter estimate/standard error of the estimate) for a t-ratio (or a Wald ratio) these variables tend to show less significance than they really have. Some of the indications of collinearity are a high R^2 with low t-ratios, or accuracy/fit drastically changes when one variable is removed. Collinearity can also switch signs which return nonsensical results. Therefore, collinearity must be tested and dealt with.

The condition index has become the gold standard in collinearity diagnostics. The condition index is the square root of the largest eigenvalue divided by each variable's eigenvalue. (An eigenvalue is the variance of each principal component when used in the correlation matrix.) The eigenvalues add up to the number of variables (including the intercept) (see Table 6.2).

This is a powerful diagnostic because a set of eigenvalues of relatively equal magnitude indicates that there is little collinearity. A small number of large eigenvalues indicates that a small number of component variables describe most of the variability of the variables. A zero eigenvalue implies perfect collinearity and – this is important – very small eigenvalues means there is severe collinearity. Note that an eigenvalue near 0.00 indicates collinearity. As a rule of thumb, a condition index > 30 indicates severe collinearity.

Common outputs along with the condition index are the proportions of variance (see Table 6.2). This proportion of variance shows the percentage of the variance of the coefficient associated with each eigenvalue. A high proportion of variance reveals a strong association with the eigenvalue.

TABLE 6.2 Collinearity diagnostics

NUMBER	EIGEN VALUE	COND INDEX	VAR PROP INTER	VAR PROP X1	VAR PROP X2	VAR PROP X3	VAR PROP X4
1	3.815	1.000	0.251	0.005	0.180	0.511	0.499
2	0.992	1.961	0.365	0.215	0.169	0.006	0.002
3	0.198	4.385	0.062	0.345	0.601	0.488	0.478
4	0.042	9.569	0.155	0.206	0.017	0.002	0.018
5	0.002	42.796	0.177	0.233	0.034	0.001	0.010

Let's talk about Table 6.2. First look at the column called condition index. The eigenvalue on the intercept is 3.815 and the first condition index is the square root of 3.815 / 3.815 = 1.00. Now the second condition index is the square root of 3.815 / 0.0992 = 1.961. The diagnostics indicate that there are as many collinearity problems as there are condition indexes > 30, or in this case there may be only one problem (42.796).

Look to the proportion of variance table. Any proportion > 0.50 is a red flag. The X2 variable has a variance proportion of 0.601 and X3 has 0.511 and also nearly an indication at 0.488. This indicates X3 is the most problematic variable and it may have some relationship with X2. Something ought to be done about that.

Corrections

Possible solutions might mean combining X2 and X3 into a factor and using the resulting factor as a variable instead of X2 and X2 as currently measured. This is because factors are by construction uncorrelated (we call it orthogonal). Another option would be to transform (especially) X3, either taking its exponent, or square root, or something else. The point is to try to find an X3-like variable correlated with the dependent variable but LESS CORRELATED with, especially, X2. Are you able to get a larger sample? Can you take differences in X3, rather than just the raw measure? And yes, if there is a theoretical reason, you can drop X3 (or X2) and re-run the model and see what you have. Dropping a variable is the last resort.

Depending on the issues, the data and other factors, other possible solutions exist. Putting all the independent variables in a factor matrix would keep the variable's variance intact but the factors are, by definition, orthogonal (uncorrelated). Of course this 'buries' any particular independent variable's impact. That is, if you are doing a demand model you very likely want to know how price impacts units, so price cannot be put in a factor.

Another (correcting) technique is ridge regression (typically using Stein estimates) and requires special software (in SAS 'proc reg data = x.x outvif outset = xx ridge = 0 to 1 by 0.01; model y = x1 x2' etc) and expertise in its use. In general, it trades collinearity for bias in the parameter estimates. Again, the balance is in knowing the coefficients are now biased but a drastic reduction in collinearity results. Is it worth it? The answer is, it depends.

Business case

So as expected Scott's boss Becky called him to her office.

'Scott, I wanted to say thanks for the demand model you did last week.'

'Well, my group did it, I just cheered them on.'

'Yes, and the output was insightful. I was able to make recommendations about marcomm effectiveness. So that was perfect.'

'Glad to help,' Scott said, knowing what was coming next.

'There were some intriguing questions about your presentation, especially around price elasticity. That generated a lot of discussion because we know we discount too much. We just don't know how to decrease our discounting, or how to target it. Not to mention, the idea of changing our discounting process scares merchandizers to death.'

'I know. All business emotions proceed from either fear or greed and merchandizers seem rooted in fear.'

Becky laughed. 'Yes, probably right. They are most worried that changing discounting, that is, changing net price, will affect their inventory forecasts.'

'I'm sure it will. But once elasticity modelling is proven, that can be an input into the forecast. That was exactly what happened at my last job.'

'And the idea that we can discount effectively, even target discounting, means we will only give away margin when we need to,' she said. 'So... ', she smiled.

'Right. Well we can design an elasticity model from our database. We will eventually do a behavioural segmentation and do elasticity for each segment, and for each major product category, if that's the right strategy. But right now let's just get an overall idea of price sensitivity.'

'Good, so what will this do for us?'

'Well, in general we'll know how sensitive our customers are to price.'

'You mentioned doing it by major product category.'

'Yes, that's probably what should be done now, at least as a first pass. Have a different model for each major product category. That is, we would estimate the price elasticity on electronics, on fashion merchandize, on toys, and so on.'

'That would be perfect,' Becky smiled. Scott nodded and headed to his office.

He sat down and was putting together an invite for his team to start thinking about elasticity modelling.

Scott sent the invite and then leaned back in his chair. His team would have some good ideas and they knew this business. None of them were high-end analytics pros though and had a lot to learn.

A few weeks went by and Scott got updates on data collections.

Then the day came when Scott's team was ready to show him the first outputs of the elasticity model. They had been working for a couple of weeks collecting data and strategizing their first attempts.

The head analyst, Mark, would lead the discussion. He plugged in the overhead projector to his laptop. Of course it did not work.

'The same thing would happen at my last place,' Scott smiled. 'Why does this thing take four or five tries to just project onto the screen?'

'It's always about getting the input connection and all that set up. I forget to push F4 or F5 or something, but eventually it works. It's even worse when we have someone on the phone. There,' Mark said. 'I think that's it.'

And it was. Mark showed Scott the output of the elasticity model, in this case for consumer electronics. 'Here is the initial output.'

Mark showed Table 6.3.

TABLE 6.3   Elasticity: model output

VARIABLE	BETA	SE	T-RATIO
# DM	0.006	0.004	1.375
# EM	−0.015	0.056	−0.268
# SMS	0.001	0.001	1.111
Q2	150.006	195.055	0.769
Q3	471.065	290.655	1.621
Q4	942.006	605.665	1.555
ADVERT	0.002	0.007	0.303
EVENTS	216.605	190.566	1.137
AVG PRICE	2.556	1.968	1.299
ADJ R^2	89.9%		

'Hmmm,' Scott said. 'What did you all think of that output?'

'Well, it fits, but very little is significant and average price is positive.'

'Right, good catch,' Scott said. 'Obvious signs of collinearity.'

Mark nodded. 'So we tested for influential observations and created another two variables to account for positive and negative outliers.'

'Is this influential diagnostics, or...?'

'No, it's just a z-score applied to the dependent variable, the quantity of consumer electronics purchased. When that variable is greater than three standard deviations away from the mean, the positive binary variable is turned from a zero to a one. Converse is true for the negative.'

'Yes, that'll work. I'll show you later the dfbeta diagnostics which are a little more powerful.'

'Dfbeta?'

'It's an interesting metric. It actually calculates the beta coefficient, on every variable, with each row subsequently removed. For example, what is the difference in the beta coefficient with row 1 in and then with row 1 out. Then what is the difference in the beta coefficient with row 2 in and then row 2 out. It produces a table for each row for each independent variable that shows the effect of that row in and out on that beta coefficient. The table can get long so we usually just graph it and when a dfbeta is greater than, say, 2.00 we look at that observation carefully, because that one row had an enormous effect on the independent variable's coefficient.'

They looked at him. Scott realized his voice had risen with his excitement. This excitement always happens to analytic people in talking about marketing science.

Scott cleared his throat. 'I'll take you through the details later, but it is great though, isn't it? Go on.'

'Then we ran multi-collinearity diagnostics, which you can see here.'

'Why do you call it multi-collinearity?' Scott asked. 'Is there any kind of collinearity that is not "multi", I mean is there such a thing as "single-collinearity"?'

The group laughed. A little. Not everyone got it.

Mark shook his head sheepishly and showed Table 6.4. 'We removed advertising, based on the correlation matrix.'

Scott sat up straight. 'You mean you removed advertising from the model?'

'Because it's correlation with the other variables is higher than anything else.'

TABLE 6.4 Correlation matrix

	# DM	# EM	# SMS	Q2	Q3	Q4	ADVERT	EVENTS	AVG PRICE
# DM	Xxx								
# EM	65%	Xxx							
# SMS	52%	67%	xxx						
Q2	-5%	-23%	1%	xxx					
Q3	11%	44%	34%	0%	xxx				
Q4	38%	69%	73%	0%	0%	xxx			
ADVERT	64%	71%	74%	74%	87%	94%	xxx		
EVENTS	-23%	88%	79%	-15%	39%	88%	69%	xxx	
AVG PRICE	13%	-22%	9%	11%	22%	-12%	-34%	9%	xxx

Scott looked around. 'We will not test collinearity based on the simple Pearson correlation coefficient, that is, the correlation matrix. And we definitely will not just drop a variable. Or do you conclude that advertising is not important in driving demand?'

'No, we do think advertising is important in driving demand.'

Scott furrowed his brow. 'But you just dropped it.'

'Well, it's obviously causing some multi... I mean some collinearity problems.'

'That may be. Can I use your laptop? Let me show you a far more insightful and instructive diagnostic. In SAS it's called VIF and we add the COLLIN option to show the condition index and the proportional variance. Here is that output.' Scott displayed Table 6.5.

'Now, the VIF is a first sign, and any variable > 10 is indicative of a potential problem. The VIF basically runs a regression using each independent variable as the dependent variable and all the other independent variables as independent variables.'

'Ah, what?'

'Say we have three independent variables: X1, X2 and X3. VIF runs a regression as X1 = X2 and X3, a second regression as X2 = X1 and X3 and lastly X3 = X1 and X2.'

'I see.'

'Any VIF greater than 10 (the formula is $1 / [1-R^2]$), that is, an $R^2 > 90\%$, means that set of variables can accurately estimate the variable as dependent, meaning there is some interaction.'

'Oh. So that shows DM and SMS as an issue.'

'Yes, a yellow flag at least. Then we use the condition index to tell how many problems there are. This does not mean which variables are necessarily problems, only the number of interdependencies. The number of condition indexes greater than 30 tells the number of problems. In this case there is one big problem. It might be several variables are interacting to create this one problem.'

They all looked at the output. 'And the variance proportion?'

'The condition index is the square root of the largest eigenvalue divided by each subsequent eigenvalue. The variance proportion shows how much variance is explained by each eigenvalue. Any greater than 50% is a red flag. So you take all these together and that usually helps point the way toward which variables are interacting enough to cause a problem.'

'Wow, that's a lot,' Mark said. 'So what does all this mean? How do we use it?'

TABLE 6.5 Model collinearity diagnostics

PRIN CMP	EIGEN VALUE	COND INDX	# DM	# EM	# SMS	ADVERT	EVENTS	AVG PRICE
1	4.550	1.000	2%	32%	5%	2%	19%	9%
2	1.090	2.043	14%	1%	2%	9%	21%	34%
3	0.311	3.825	1%	2%	11%	20%	0%	24%
4	0.029	12.526	2%	62%	64%	2%	26%	16%
5	0.017	16.360	59%	2%	14%	19%	13%	15%
6	0.003	38.944	22%	1%	3%	48%	21%	2%
VIF			43.11	8.54	29.55	8.55	2.88	5.15

'Well, it's a bit of an art as well as science, but real modelling always is. I would say the VIF tells us marcomm looks to be a problem, and it's no surprise they are correlated. Then the condition index tells us we have one interdependency, that is, there is one dimension that is so interdependent that it is ill-conditioned, meaning it's bad enough to correct. The variance proportion says that each of the marcomm variables are greater than 50%.'

'So what do we do about it?'

'Note that we do not just drop a variable. Advertising is important in explaining the movement of units and yes it has some correlation to at least one other variable. The common corrections are ridge regression and factor analysis. That would be my suggestion. Here, let's run factor analysis on all the variables except price.'

'What will that do?'

'A factor is by mathematic construction perfectly UNcorrelated with the other factors. We can drastically reduce the interdependency of the factors and measure the effect of price on its own. That means we will run a regression as:

$$\text{Units} = f(\text{Factor 1, Factor 2, Factor n, price}).$$

'Hopefully this will remove most of the damaging collinearity and we can then calculate price elasticity. Price should have a negative coefficient.'

Mark reached for his laptop. 'Here is average price and average quantity for consumer electronics. Average price is 26.5 and average quantity is 15.35. With the new price coefficient of -0.765 elasticity calculates as -1.32, making it sensitive to price.'

'Yes,' said Scott. 'Mildly. That's probably to be expected?'

The group nodded.

'OK, let's move on to the next category.'

After they went through all the major product categories they had an estimate of price elasticity for each. This would tell them for which categories they should discount heavily and which they should not.

Next quarter they would go through a behavioural segmentation project that would estimate elasticity by product, by segment. That is, one segment might be sensitive to the price of consumer electronics and another segment might NOT be sensitive to the price of consumer electronics. This implies targeting and personalization. Talk about fun!

Conclusion

Elasticity modelling is a rarely done but strategically critical analysis for any retail firm. Understanding and quantifying those levers that drive units is a necessary requirement for any marketer.

Quantifying how sensitive units are to a movement in an independent variable (price, marcomm, etc) should be the first step in marketing analytics. Elasticity is typically done at least in terms of price. This is because knowing where a firm is operating on the demand curve, either the elastic or inelastic portion, lets them know in which direction to change price in order to increase total revenue. On the inelastic demand curve total revenue follows price so in order to increase total revenue price should be raised. If operations are on the elastic portion of the demand curve total revenue follows units and (since price and units are inversely related) to increase total revenue means lowering price so units will increase.

Checklist

You'll be the smartest person in the room if you:

☐ Advocate the strategic power of modelling elasticity.

☐ Remember that there are two major types of elasticity: inelastic and elastic (technically a third type is called unitary elasticity). Inelastic demand means that for an X per cent change in price there is less than X per cent change in units. An elastic demand curve means that for an X per cent change in price there is a greater than X per cent change in units.

☐ Point out that there is an inverse relationship between price and units.

☐ Educate your peers that while price and units are negatively correlated (price goes up, units go down) the real actionability is what happens to total revenue. In an inelastic demand curve total revenue follows price. That is, as price goes up (units go down) and total revenue goes UP, meaning that in order to increase total revenue on the inelastic portion of the demand curve prices have to be RAISED. In an elastic demand curve total revenue follows units. That is, as price goes up (units go down) and total revenue goes DOWN, meaning that in order

▶

to increase total revenue on the elastic portion of the demand curve prices have to be DECREASED.

☐ Never do demand modelling with a log–log model. That is, taking the natural log of all variables (eg units, price) explicitly assumes a constant elasticity which, while it makes the mathematics easier also makes little (marketing) sense.

VALUING   07
MARKETING
COMMUNICATIONS
(MARCOMM)

MARKETING QUESTION

How can I value marcomm? Where should I invest marcomm spend?

ANALYTIC SOLUTION

Ordinary regression using polynomial distributed lags (PDL)

Marcomm is what we call marketing communications. It typically means direct marketing communications, meaning direct mail, e-mail, SMS. That is, it is targeted. This means there has to be a known and correct address to which to send the communication.

    The issue with marcomm, beyond targeting, is that expenses differ by channel. Direct mail is obviously expensive while e-mail is not. (E-mail is not expensive in terms of financial cost but as will be seen there is also the 'e-mail fatigue' issue, which basically means that a firm has sent someone so many irrelevant or unwanted e-mails so often that the customer just opts out or ignores them. Even when they might be of value. This cost is more abstract but just as important.) What this means is that understanding the return on investment (ROI) of marcomm by channel is critical to success. To know how effective each channel is will help in allocating budget.

Note this is not the same thing as 'media mix modelling'. Media mix modelling (MMM) is typically about ALL media, including TV, radio and billboards. It is also about the interaction of all media with other variables – more appropriately called marketing mix modelling – which adds price, season, channel, etc. MMM always has a lag structure and this lag structure is usually distributed, often along a polynomial function, called PDL. MMM can be a system of equations and the dependent variable is usually units or maybe transactions.

What we're talking about doing here is ordinary regression and we are measuring the impact of marcomm on revenue. Revenue is units multiplied by price so price is not (cannot be) an independent variable. The insight from marcomm valuation is to quantify what percentage of revenue is driven by each (direct) marcomm vehicle. This has strategic budgeting implications. For example, if you know that 15 per cent of revenue is driven by direct mail, would you put more than 15 per cent of your budget in direct mail? Maybe, if you realized the elasticity was > 1.00. But that is where analytics helps.

So, the general form of the model is:

$$Revenue = f(direct\ mail,\ e\text{-}mail,\ SMS,\ etc)$$

Seasonality can be included, and consumer confidence and other things. The model is a time series model so serial correlation will have to be diagnosed and corrected as appropriate.

In terms of the marcomm variables, ideally they would be measured in spend so the insights would be in the same terms. This is what marketing managers need: budget implications. That is, you would be able to say, 'An increase in direct mail spend of X will drive, on average, an increase in revenue of Y'. The other option (and probably easier to collect) is number of marcomm sent. That is, in time period 1 we sent 110,000 direct mail pieces, and 350,000 e-mails. Because the model is about the amount of direct mail, both revenue and cost are known. This gives insights into how direct mail drives ROI. Both methods work fine.

Another issue to mention before we get to the business case is the issue of distributed lags. It is accepted that the impact of a marcomm stimulus is not immediately felt nor does it immediately dissipate. That is, the distributed impact is lagged. Figure 7.1 shows the typical hypothesized structure, in this case a polynomial lag of 5 degrees. To interpret, let's assume we dropped a large quantity of direct mail at Time 1, and each lag is one week. At Time 1 we get 10 per cent of the impact on revenue, at Time 2, 26 per cent, at Time 3, 37 per cent, etc, until by the 6th week the impact (of that direct mail drop) essentially dissipates to zero. Now, isn't it great that we can: 1) estimate how a particular marcomm drop affects demand/revenue; and 2) show its amplitude/lag impact as well? That's why we're in analytics!

FIGURE 7.1   Distributed lag impact

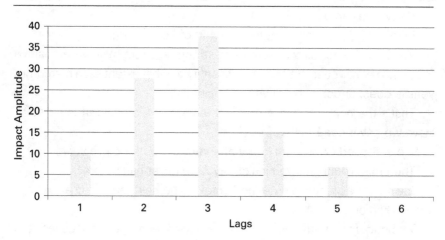

The modelling aspects of this technique are fairly direct.

Business case

The director of marcomm, Cassandra, walked into Scott's office. She had an advertising and brand background, something that usually meant she and Scott did not talk the same language. Or even use the same alphabet.

So Scott was surprised she was cordial to him, given their differences. But he also knew that she needed him and his analytic skills.

And Scott knew she was there to talk about her marcomm budget: how she could manage the budget given it was always under pressure to show value and was always scrutinized to be cut.

'So I need to understand what impact marcomm spend has on revenue,' she said, pursing her lips. 'Is there a way to know how different investment will drive our business?'

'Hmmm,' Scott mused. 'The easiest would be to do a time series model of marcomm valuation.'

She looked at him.

'By that I mean we might be able to quantify the impact of each major marcomm vehicle and estimate its lagged effect on revenue.'

'Lagged...?'

'Yes, the idea is that a million catalogues dropped on 1 January would not only impact 1 January, but that revenue impact would be distributed, lagged over time.'

'Wow, you can do that?'

'In theory,' Scott smiled, getting a whiff of her perfume.

'Will I be able to tell that some investment in direct mail has a positive ROI, while e-mail does not? Can you quantify to what extent each marcomm vehicle does, or does not, drive the business?'

'That's the goal. There are many caveats, but we could at least start. Have we never done that before?'

She shrugged. 'Not that I know of and I've been here five years.'

'Then this would give you insights you've never had before.'

She smiled a practised smile and unfolded herself from the chair, waved and walked out.

So Scott met with his team of analysts and they discussed the business objective and modelling framework. The group dynamics were changing, becoming a little more thoughtful and a little more confident. Scott was seen as a cheerleader as much as a subject matter expert. Which was just what he intended.

'So the obvious technique is a dependent-type analysis, some kind of regression,' Scott said.

The group nodded, knowing something was coming.

Scott smiled and went to the white board and wrote:

$$\text{Revenue} = f(\text{marcomm, price, season, other})$$

'What about this?'

'We would get a measure of how marcomm – whatever we mean by that – is in terms of driving revenue, which is what she wants,' Mark said.

'Yes. But...?'

'Since revenue = price * units we cannot have price as both an independent variable and part of the dependent variable.'

Scott smiled.

'So, maybe we change the dependent variable to be units instead?'

'But we want to measure revenue; we want to put all the valuation in terms of revenue.'

Mark shrugged.

FIGURE 7.2   Hypothesized marketing mix model

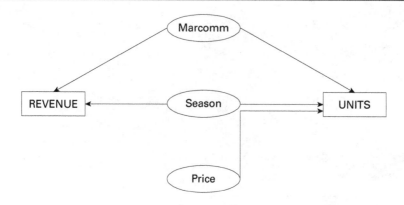

Scott then drew Figure 7.2 on the white board. 'We need to account for the cross-equation correlation, that is, revenue measured as units multiplied by price, and marcomm and season impact units and revenue. That is, we need to measure these simultaneously.'

The group looked at each other.

'And that's not all. We need to account for the fact that the impact of marcomm is not felt all at once or even immediately, but is distributed and lagged.'

Now the group looked stricken.

'And since it's time series,' Mark worried, 'what about autocorrelation?'

'Sure, that has to be diagnosed and corrected. Relax,' Scott laughed. 'I'll help. It'll be fun.'

Scott explained how SAS and most other programs had a module for simultaneous equations and putting in a lag structure. (If nothing else, manually lagging the variables will work, if necessary.)

So Scott's gang worked with simultaneous equations (3SLS) to account for price indirectly impacting revenue and marcomm and seasonality directly impacting revenue. The output (of the revenue model) is shown in Table 7.1.

TABLE 7.1   Marcomm valuation

	COEFF	MEANS	VALUE	% OF REV
INT	16.911	1.00	16.91	20%
EM1	−0.11	34.72	−3.82	−5%
EM2	0.12	30.01	3.60	4%
DM1	0.38	73.06	27.76	33%
DM2	0.06	294.66	17.68	21%
SMS	2.55	4.34	11.07	13%
Q4	18.9	0.25	4.73	6%
Q3	12.2	0.25	3.05	4%
Q2	9.64	0.25	2.41	3%
		AVG SPEND 83.39		100%

The COEFF column shows the beta parameter estimate of each variable. The MEANS column shows the average of each variable. This tells on average how many of each type of marcomm was sent: ie for EM1 34.72 were sent to each customer (yes, that's a lot of e-mails!). The next column VALUE multiplies the coefficient estimate by the average of each variable to calculate a total impact on revenue. Note that on average each customer spent 83.39.

Now let's look at SMS. The coefficient is 2.55 and on average 4.34 communications were sent. This results in 11.07 total impact to total revenue, which is 13%. That is, of the 83.39 total average revenue, 13% tends to come from using SMS. Pay particular attention to EM1. Using the same calculation EM1 actually DECREASES total revenue. This is often the case with e-mail fatigue.

A very obvious business case/ROI can be calculated from the above model. For example, we send 73.06 DM1 and its estimated impact on total revenue is 27.76. Say that the cost per piece is 0.35, or 73.06 * 0.35 = 25.57. So the ROI is 8.6% (27.76 – 25.57)/25.57.

The other very cool and very useful output of the marcomm valuation model is the estimated PDL, polynomial distributed lag. This is in recognition of the fact that the impact of some independent variables (especially stimuli like marcomm) typically last over a period of time and the impact has a shape. This structure can be modelled. Scott's team did this very thing and found the following output, shown in Figure 7.3.

FIGURE 7.3   E-mail (1), polynomial distributed lag impact

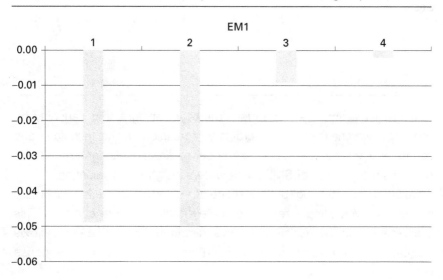

Figure 7.3 shows the distributed lag impact from EM1. It's negative and sums to –0.11. It tends to last four periods. Figure 7.4 shows DM1 that sums to 0.38 with a longer period lag. Knowing the shape and length of impact has strategic implications, especially in terms of manipulating the sales cycle, particularly trying to flatten out the demand response. Now how cool is that!?

FIGURE 7.4   Direct mail (1), polynomial distributed lag impact

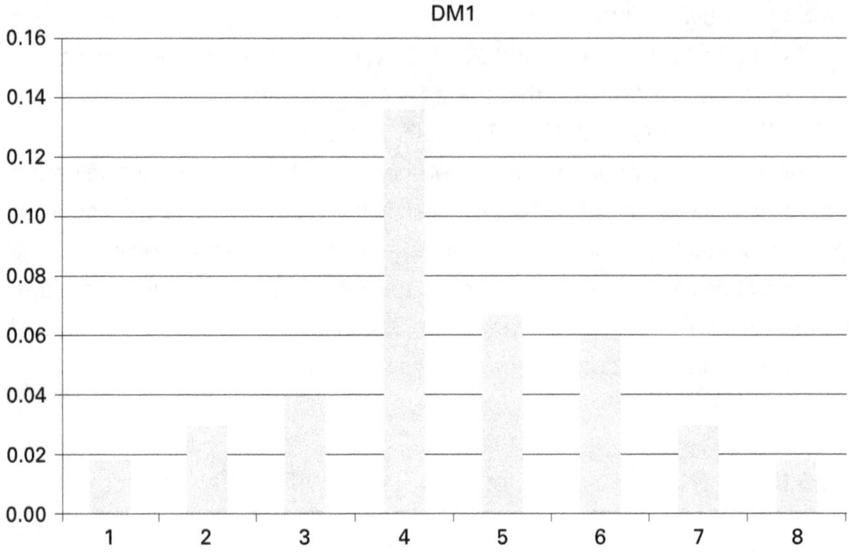

Conclusion

Valuing marcomm is an important marketing insight that can only be quantified via analytics. Using ordinary regression as the technique and counts of marcomm stimuli – the number of direct mails sent, number of e-mails sent, number of SMS sent – allows insights into valuation.

Valuation is one thing, but the shape of the impact curve is much more interesting. Modelling a response curve should be more common. This chapter showed the use of polynomial distributed lags (PDL) that allows insights into both amplitude, shape and length of the stimuli's response curve.

Checklist

You'll be the smartest person in the room if you:

☐ Advocate using marcomm valuation as a technique that is probably superior to A/B testing.

☐ Use marcomm valuation with counts of stimuli as independent variables giving the estimate of ROI. That is, the estimated units from the dependent variable can be multiplied by average price (generating revenue) and the cost of marcomm should be known. This will give a business case with marcomm spend impacting estimated revenue.

☐ Keep in mind that one advantage of PDL is that not only does it value marcomm but implies and estimates a distribution length (ie shape of the impact) and these insights can be very powerful.

FORECASTING
FUTURE DEMAND

08

MARKETING QUESTION

How can I forecast demand?

ANALYTIC SOLUTION

Autoregression and/or ARIMA

Forecasting demand is often not a marketing function, but resides more in merchandize or operations, even finance. Either way, it is an important analysis on which retailers depend.

Just as investment analysis has two schools of thought to predict stock prices (technical and fundamental) so are there two philosophies of forecasting: those based on causality and those not based on causality. Regression-like techniques are based on causality (this causes that) and all other techniques are not based on causality. The non-causality types range from simplistic (eg exponential smoothing, moving averages) to the very sophisticated (ARIMA).

Autocorrelation

Forecasting tends to use time series data. As such, auto (serial) correlation is always a potential problem. Autocorrelation is when the error terms are correlated with each other. Very common is 1st-order autocorrelation, which occurs when consecutive errors are correlated. Generally, if the data is daily, there can be a 7th-order autocorrelation, if the data is monthly there can be a 12th-order autocorrelation, etc. We write 1st-order auto-correlation as AR(1).

Remember, one of the assumptions of ordinary regression is no serial correlation. A violation of this assumption means that, while the parameter estimates are unbiased, they are inefficient. Autocorrelation also means the standard errors are biased, and they are typically biased downward. This means the t-ratio ($\beta/se\beta$) will be artificially higher than it should be, meaning the independent variable will appear to be more significant than it really is.

Diagnosis of autocorrelation is generally easy: the Durbin–Watson test is standard (for AR(1) process). The DW statistic tests the null hypothesis of no 1st-order autocorrelation. A couple of comments are important in interpreting DW. First, let's note extreme values of correlation (ρ). If $\rho = 1$ then DW = 0, if $\rho = -1$ then DW = 4 and if $\rho = 0$ then DW = 2. There is an indeterminate region on either side of positive and negative correlation so the DW table is of utmost use in cases where DW is close (how close is close?) to 2.00, which is the ideal metric.

Correcting for AR(1) is also rather straightforward. The process is called Cochrane–Orcutt procedure. It essentially estimates and re-estimates correlation of subsequent errors over and over until the correlation estimate does not change. Then, once estimated correlation is known, a technique called quasi-differencing is applied and DW is used to see if autocorrelation has been eliminated.

To estimate ρ:

1 Run OLS and collect the error terms.

2 Regress the error terms on lagged one-period values:

    a That is, $e = \rho e_{t-1} + w$.

3 Re-run OLS using quasi-differencing:

- Lag the data to get Y_{t-1} and X_{t-1}
- Multiply the lagged values using estimated ρ:

$$\rho Y_{t-1} \text{ and } \rho X_{t-1}$$

- Create Quasi-differencing variables:

$$Y^*_t = Y_t - \rho Y_{t-1}, \ X^*_t = X_t - \rho X_{t-1}$$

- Run OLS (now referred to as GLS, for generalized least squares) on the new data

4 Now regress again from above GLS $e = \rho e_{t-1} + w$.

5 Continue until successive iteration creates no change in the estimated ρ.

This method will essentially eliminate autocorrelation and the DW should be approximately 2.00.

Dummy variables and seasonality

Dummy variables (more appropriately called binary variables) are those independent variables that have two values, 0 or 1. They show up in a lot of applications: eg did this customer get this stimulus (=1) or not (=0)? was this programme in effect for this time period (=1), or not (=0)? It is a very common way to account for seasonality.

To account for seasonality, assume we have monthly data and want to account for a quarterly effect. The data-set would look like Table 8.1. When we are actually in Q1, the variable called Q1 is 'turned on' and when we are not in Q1 that variable is 'turned off'.

Why are binary variables commonly called dummy variables? I would guess it's because of the dummy trap. For example, if you use the above seasonal data and use all four variables, the sum of each row is always equal to 1, ie there is no variance. The algorithm will not solve, and will explode and the software will give you an insulting message. The solution is to drop one of the variables, say Q1. Then the interpretation of the remaining variables is in relation to the dropped variable. That is, if the coefficient on Q2 is 225, you can say that Q2 has an impact on the dependent variable of 225 more than Q1. Thus it is typical to use dummy variables to account for seasonality.

TABLE 8.1   Seasonal dummy variables

Month	Q1	Q2	Q3	Q4
Jan	1	0	0	0
Feb	1	0	0	0
Mar	1	0	0	0
Apr	0	1	0	0
May	0	1	0	0
Jun	0	1	0	0
Jul	0	0	1	0
Aug	0	0	1	0
Sep	0	0	1	0
Oct	0	0	0	1
Nov	0	0	0	1
Dec	0	0	0	1

A quick departure about something that sometimes gets in the way in terms of forecasting discussions. Forecasting is about making a prediction (especially of the dependent variable) for some time period in the future, eg a period of time we have not experienced yet. That is often called a prediction. Thinking about the time period we have in our data, that is, the known (actual) values of the dependent (and independent) variables, when we do ordinary regression, for example, we have a predicted dependent variable. In truth this should be called an 'estimated', not predicted, value of the dependent variable. But it's also true that these irritating misnomers only come up in a forecasting conversion. Along with where the stock market is going and picking the winner of the Super Bowl/World Series.

Business case

Scott knew the next step of the demand model would be to forecast demand. He had not had too much forecasting in his past and hoped some of his team members had a better background.

But none of them did.

'OK, Mark, you put together the model itself and I'll find some way to forecast the independent variables.'

Scott leafed through some textbooks he had and paid attention to forecasting techniques. He thought about ARIMA (autoregressive integrated moving averages), the very famous approach from Box–Jenkins. He liked a lot about it: for example, there were several diagnostics, and it was easy to interpret and explain. It appeared very sophisticated. What he did not like about it was that it was not causal, it did not specify THIS causes THAT, which was something Scott tried to make all analytics conform to. If a cause cannot be quantified its use is hard to justify. He especially did not like the very analytic approaches that did not included causality. It seemed to him like window dressing, like pounding the pulpit very hard when the point is actually quite weak. The idea was that if the technique was NOT going to be causal, sophistication was of no value. He dismissed ARIMA.

He decided to do some kind of moving averages. While both ARIMA and moving averages are non-causality-based, Scott thought the over-sophistication of ARIMA did not work for this project. The details gave others a confidence that the algorithm did not deserve, that is, they trusted the output because of (overly engineered?) analytics. He would have to forecast net price and marcomm, each of which are tied to seasonality – especially marcomm. Table 8.2 shows the data and Figure 8.1 charts the average number of e-mails sent per week.

He decided to use a simple moving average on the marcomm. He would take a 3-period moving average and a 13-period moving average and apply 50% to each in order to come up with the next period's forecast.

FIGURE 8.1   Average number of emails per week

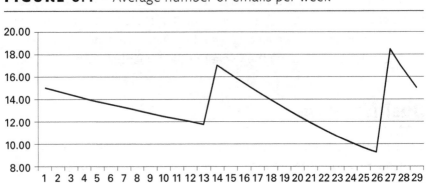

TABLE 8.2   Moving average predictions

	Avg EM	3_MA	13_MA	PRED
week1	15.00			
week2	14.70			
week3	14.41			
week4	14.12	14.70		
week5	13.84	14.41		
week6	13.56	14.12		
week7	13.29	13.84		
week8	13.02	13.56		
week9	12.76	13.29		
week10	12.51	13.02		
week11	12.26	12.76		
week12	12.01	12.51		
week13	11.77	12.26		
week14	17.00	12.01	13.33	12.67
week15	16.15	13.59	13.48	13.54
week16	15.34	14.97	13.59	14.28
week17	14.58	16.16	13.66	14.91
week18	13.85	15.36	13.70	14.53
week19	13.15	14.59	13.70	14.14
week20	12.50	13.86	13.67	13.76
week21	11.87	13.17	13.61	13.39
week22	11.28	12.51	13.52	13.01
week23	10.71	11.88	13.40	12.64
week24	10.18	11.29	13.27	12.28

TABLE 8.2 *continued*

	Avg EM	3_MA	13_MA	PRED
week25	9.67	10.72	13.11	11.92
week26	9.19	10.19	12.93	11.56
week27	18.50	9.68	12.73	11.2
week28	16.65	12.45	12.84	12.65
week29	14.99	14.78	12.88	13.83
PRED30	14.78	16.71	12.85	14.78
PRED31	14.17	15.47	12.87	14.17
PRED32	13.77	14.65	12.90	13.77

Table 8.2 shows PRED30, that is, the prediction for the 30th week. Scott averaged the previous three periods together (27, 28 and 29) to get 16.71 and then weeks 17–29 to average 12.85. The average of THESE two moving averages is 14.78. Thus 14.78 is the predicted week 30 and that is used to make the next forecast, of week 31.

Now Scott had a simple way to forecast all of the independent variables, depending what model Mark came up with. Obviously he does not have to forecast seasonality, that is, if Mark uses quarterly dummy variables they KNOW when these occur so if they are independent variables those are already usable.

'Let me show you the final model,' Mark said, smiling and showing Table 8.3.

'All of the marcomm is significant, price is negative and the fit is not bad.'

'Yes,' Scott smiled. 'I think this will work. We can easily forecast the marcomm and price with moving averages. Did you lag the variables for autocorrelation?'

'Yes, I can show that. A 5-week lag worked the best, which seems right given a weekly model.'

'Good. And e-mails are negative?'

They all looked at each other.

TABLE 8.3 Model output

	# E-MAILS	# DIR MAILS	# SMS	NET PRICE	Q2	Q3	Q4	INT
COEFF	−0.055	0.255	0.379	−0.788	15,423	38,965	41,255	18,954
SE	0.027363	0.08557	0.110174	0.173339	5175.503	10335.54	2835.395	
TRATIO	2.01	2.98	3.44	4.546	2.98	3.77	14.55	
Adj R^2	78%							

'Well...' Mark began.

'No, we find what we find. This is e-mail fatigue staring us in the face. We've found this before. The more e-mails we send the fewer units we sell. That's a powerful – if difficult to deliver – message.'

'Yep. We thought you would be the one to deliver that message.'

They all laughed. Except Scott, who knew Mark was right.

Conclusion

Forecasting demand is more an economic than a marketing exercise, but is often done out of necessity. The first decision the analysts must make is whether to model based on causality or not.

ARIMA is a powerful technique but does not rely on explaining WHY the dependent variable moves the way it does, only that the past pattern is forecasted to continue into the future.

There are a host of econometric techniques based on causality (eg autoregression) that are time series in nature. These independent variables are often macroeconomic in nature and give marketers no insights into what levers can be pulled to affect the forecast.

There are simple extensions of the dependent variable to use in coming up with a forecast for the dependent variable. These are things like exponential smoothing, moving averages, decomposition (eg trend, season, cycle). Again, these are shown only so that marketing analytics can create a forecast, even though there is no causality behind it.

Checklist

You'll be the smartest person in the room if you:

☐ Keep in mind that a forecast is different to a prediction. A forecast estimates the future value of the dependent variable (typically by predicting the independent variables that cause the movement in the dependent variable) while a prediction is an estimate of the dependent variable within the sample time frame without trying to predict future value of independent or dependent variables.

☐ Remember to test and correct for autocorrelation.

☐ Realize that it's possible to generate a forecast without having a theory of causality.

☐ Take a simplified view of forecasting as projecting independent variables via exponential smoothing, moving averages, etc, and then use them as inputs into, say, a regression-kind of model.

TARGETING THE ＲＩＧＨＴ ＣＵＳＴＯＭＥＲＳ   09

MARKETING QUESTION

Which customers are most likely to purchase? How do I target?

ANALYTIC SOLUTION

Logistic regression

Introduction

Now let's talk about targeting the probability to purchase. In many ways this is the fundamental question in all of marketing: who is likely to buy, how do I target them, how do I increase the probability for them to buy? The typical analytic technique involved is logistic regression.

Logistic regression has a lot of similarities to ordinary regression. They both have a dependent variable, they both have independent variables, they are both single equations and they both have diagnostics around the impact of independent variables on the dependent variable as well as 'fit' diagnostics.

But their differences are also many. Logistic regression has a dependent variable that takes on only two (as opposed to continuous) values: 0 or 1, that is, it's binary. Logistic regression does not use the criterion of 'minimizing the sum of the squared errors' (which is ordinary least squares, OLS) to calculate the coefficients, but rather maximum likelihood. The interpretation of the coefficients is different. Odds ratios (e^β) are typically used and fit is not about a predicted vs. an actual dependent variable. Another difference between logistic regression and ordinary regression is that logistic regression actually models the 'logit' rather than the dependent variable. A logit is: $\ln[(event) / (1 - event)]$, that is, the (natural) log of the odds of the event occurring.

By the way, there is a technique that can model a dependent variable with more than two values, but not so many as to be continuous. That is, the dependent variable might have three or four or five or more values. This technique is called multinomial logit. (In SAS we usually use PROC CATMOD for multinomial logit.) All of the above means that the output of logistic regression is a probability between 0 per cent and 100 per cent, whereas the output of ordinary regression is an estimated (predicted) value to fit the actual dependent variable. Figure 9.1 shows a plot of actual events (the 0s and the 1s) as well as the logistic (s-curve).

This is why we use logistic regression rather than ordinary regression, to bound the top and bottom values at 0 per cent and 100 per cent. If we used OLS we could get a value greater than 100 per cent and less than 0 per cent, which would be nonsensical. Now let's look at some data and run a model, because that's where all the fun is.

Business case

Scott called his team into his office.

'Folks, marketing, specifically marcomm, tells me the response rates of our catalogues has peaked. We send out 1 or 2 million catalogues a month and they've been using RFM and want to see if we can help better target.'

'Just what is meant by response rate?'

FIGURE 9.1   Logistic curve

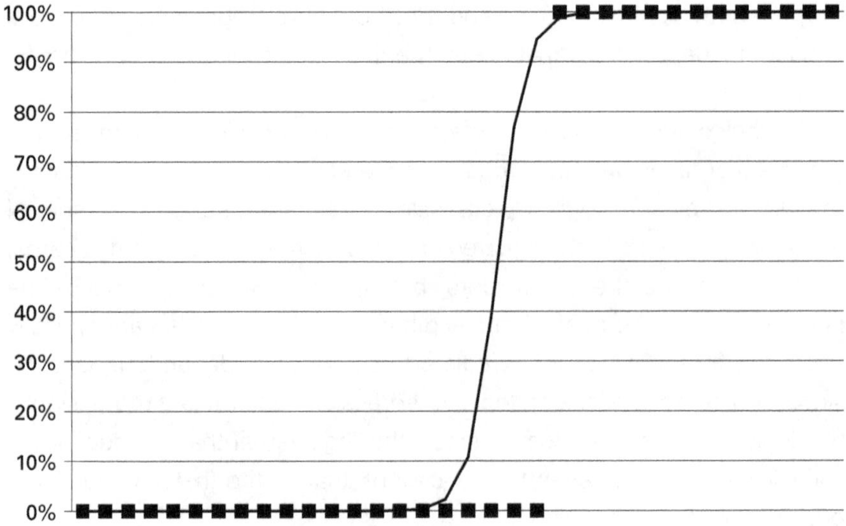

'Response rate is the rate of response, which is the number of those that responded (purchased), divided by the total number that got the communication. It's an overall metric of success. We want to target those likely to purchase based on a collection of characteristics. We have both customers and non-customers in our database – from the subscriber lists we've been mailing – so we could model the probability to respond based on clone or look-alike modelling.'

'What does that mean?' Mark asked.

'It means logistic regression. Have we used it?'

'Not really. Like you said, they pick their own lists, typically RFM or some tree structure, but you're talking about doing a model.'

'Right. When we're done, their lists can be picked by probability of each customer to purchase overall, or purchase a particular product or even a particular volume of spend. We can sort the database by probability to purchase and only mail as deep as ROI limits.'

'Sounds good. We'll look into it.'

Results applied to the model

Table 9.1 shows the simplified data-set Scott's team used. This is a list of customers who purchased and a list of those who did not.

TABLE 9.1 Dataset example

ID	Revenue	Purchase	campaign a	campaign b	campaign c	income	size hh	educ
999	1500	1	1	0	1	150000	1	19
1001	1400	1	1	0	1	137500	1	19
1003	1250	1	1	0	0	125000	2	15
1005	1100	1	1	0	0	112500	2	13
1007	2100	1	0	1	0	145000	3	16
1009	849	1	0	0	0	132500	3	17
1010	750	1	0	0	0	165000	3	16
1011	700	1	0	0	0	152500	3	9
1013	550	1	1	0	1	140000	4	15
1015	850	1	1	0	1	127500	4	18

TABLE 9.1 *continued*

ID	Revenue	Purchase	campaign a	campaign b	campaign c	income	size hh	educ
1017	450	1	1	0	1	115000	4	17
1019	0	0	0	0	1	102500	5	16
1021	0	0	0	0	1	99000	6	15
1023	0	0	0	1	1	86500	7	16
1025	0	0	0	1	1	74000	6	15
1027	0	0	0	1	1	61500	5	14
1029	0	0	0	1	1	49000	4	13
1033	0	0	1	0	1	111000	4	12
1034	0	0	0	0	1	98500	3	11
1035	0	0	0	0	1	86000	3	10

Scott has data on which campaigns each group received, as well as some demographics. The objective is to figure out which of the non-purchasers 'look like' those that did purchase and re-mail them, perhaps with the same campaign (if we find one that was effective) or design another campaign. This is why logistic regression, especially in a CRM/database marketing context, is called clone modelling.

The end result will be to score the database with 'probability to purchase' in order to understand what (statistically) works and strategize what to do next time. This is the cornerstone of direct (database) marketing.

Table 9.2 shows the output of the coefficients. These coefficients are not interpreted the same way as in ordinary regression.

TABLE 9.2 Coefficients: model output

Intercept	−57.9
Campaign a	−8.48
Campaign b	16.52
Campaign c	−9.96
Income	0.001
Size hh	−3.41
Education	0.2

Because logistic regression is curvilinear and bound by 0 and 1, the impact of the independent variables affects the dependent variable differently. The actual impact is:

$$e \wedge \text{coefficient.}$$

For example, education's coefficient is 0.200. The impact would be $e^{.200} = 1.225$, that is $(2.71828 \wedge .200)$.

This means that for every year of added education, the increase in probability is 22.5%. This metric is called the odds ratio. This obviously has targeting implications: aim our product at the highest educated families. Note that two of the three campaigns are negative (which tend to decrease probability to purchase) so this also adds credence to needing better targeting.

For logistic regression, there is not really a goodness-of-fit measure, like R^2 in OLS. Logit has a probability output between a dependent variable of 1 and 0. Often the 'confusion matrix' is used, and predictive accuracy is a sign of a good model. Table 9.3 shows the confusion matrix of the above model. (The confusion matrix from SAS uses 'c-table' as an option.)

TABLE 9.3   Confusion matrix

	Actual non-events	**Actual events**
Predicted non-events	1,000	1,750
Predicted events	500	6,750

Say there are 10,000 observations. The total number of events (purchases) is 6,750 + 1,750 or 8,500. The model predicted only 6,750 + 500 or 7,250. The total accuracy of the model is the actual events predicted correctly and the actual non-events predicted correctly, meaning 6,750 + 1,000 or 7,750 / 10,000 = 77.5%. The number of false positives is 500 (the model predicted 500 people would have the event that did not: this is an important measure of direct marketing, in terms of the cost of a wrong mailing).

It often helps to determine if the dependent variable (sales, in this case) has any abnormal observations. Remember the z-score? This is a fast and simple way to check if an observation is 'out of bounds'. The z-score is calculated as ((observation – mean) / standard deviation). Let's say the mean of revenue is 358.45 and the standard deviation of revenue is 569.72. So, if you run this calculation for all the observations on revenue you will see that (Table 9.1) ID # 1007 ((2100 – 358.45) / 569.72) = 3.074. This means that observation is > 3 standard deviations from the mean, a very non-normal observation. It is common to add a new variable, call it 'positive outlier' and it will take the value of 0 as long as the z-score on sales is < 3.00, then it takes the value of 1 if z-score > 3. Use this new variable as another independent variable to help account for outliers. Some of the coefficients should change and the fit usually improves. This new variable can be seen as an influential observation.

Note the slight changes in coefficients in Table 9.4. This ought to mean accuracy increases. Then note the updated confusion matrix in Table 9.5.

TABLE 9.4   Model coefficients

Intercept	−51.9
Influence	15.54
Campaign a	−6.06
Campaign b	16.6
Campaign c	−9.07
Income	0.002
Size HH	−1.65
Education	0.211

TABLE 9.5   Updated confusion matrix

	Actual non-events	**Actual events**
Predicted non-events	1,250	1,000
Predicted events	250	7,500

The total number of events (purchases) is still 8,500 but note the shift in accuracy. The model now predicts 7,500 + 250 = 7,750. The total accuracy of the model is the actual events predicted correctly and the actual non-events predicted correctly, meaning 7,500 + 1,250 or 8,750 / 10,000 = 87.5%. The number of false positives is 250: the model predicted 250 people would have the event that did not: this is an important measure of direct marketing, in terms of the cost of a wrong mailing. The model improved because of accounting for influential observations.

Scott liked what he saw. 'Yes, this'll work,' he said. 'Good job.'

'We'll get this into production this week and help marcomm start pulling their targeted lists.'

'Good. I like the way you used the z-score to detect and correct influential observations.'

They all stopped and looked at him; they knew he was about to make a suggestion.

'A more involved and rigorous technique is to use studentized residuals and remove those observations that are greater than 3 standard deviations.

That is, rather than apply the z-score to one variable, say the dependent variable, apply the z-score to the error term, the residual. This will take into account the whole model, rather than just the distribution of only one variable.'

'Essentially standardizing the residuals? Then accounting for those observations that are outliers?'

'Yes, just one step beyond what you already did. So-called studentized residuals take into account the whole model, that's the benefit. Three standard deviations should account for less than one-tenth of one per cent.'

They nodded and smiled. Scott liked his new job.

A brief procedural note

On probably most of the analytic techniques we'll talk about, certain assumptions are built in. That is, regression has many assumptions about linearity, normality, etc. This means that in reality, for every regression technique used, every assumption should be checked and every violation of assumptions should be tested for and corrected, if possible. This goes for OLS, logit and anything else. OK?

Variable diagnostics

As in all regression, a significance test is performed on the independent variables but because logit is non-linear, the t-test becomes the Wald test (which is the t-test squared, so $1.96^2 = 3.84$, at 95%). The p-value still needs to be < 0.05.

Pseudo-R^2

Logistic regression does not have an R^2 statistic. This intimidates a lot of people but that's why I showed the 'confusion matrix' which is a measure of goodness of fit. Remember (from OLS) R^2 is the shared variance between the actual dependent variable and the predicted dependent variable. The more variance these two share, the closer the predicted and actual dependent variables are. Remember OLS outputs an estimated dependent variable. Logistic regression does NOT output an estimated dependent variable. The actual dependent variable is 0 or 1. The 'logit' is the natural log of the event / (1 – event). So there can be no 'estimated' dependent variable. If you HAVE to have some measure of goodness of fit I'd suggest using the log likelihood on the covariate and intercept. SPSS and SAS both output the –2LL on the intercept only and the –2LL of the intercept and covariates. Think of the –2LL on intercept as TSS (total sum of squares) and –2LL on intercept and covariates as RSS (regression sum of squares). R^2 is RSS/TSS and this will give an indicated (called a pseudo-R^2) for those that need that metric.

Conclusion

Logistic regression is a fundamental analytic technique. Because so much of marketing (and analytics) is about choice behaviour and those choices are often a yes or no decision, having a technique that gives probability to make the decision is very powerful.

Checklist

You'll be the smartest person in the room if you:

☐ Can differentiate between logistic and ordinary regression. Logistic and ordinary regression is similar in that both are single equations having a dependent variable explained by one or more independent variables. They are dissimilar in that ordinary regression has a continuous dependent variable while logistic regression has a binary variable; ordinary regression uses least squares to estimate the coefficients while logistic regression uses maximum likelihood.

☐ Remember that logistic regression predicts a probability of an event.

☐ Point out that the 'confusion matrix' is a means of goodness of fit.

☐ Suggest logistic regression as a way to model market baskets.

MAXIMIZING THE   10
IMPACT OF MAILING

MARKETING QUESTION

How deep should the (direct) mailing be?

ANALYTIC SOLUTION

Logistic regression and lift/gain charts

Introduction

Direct marketers especially always need to know, 'How deep do I mail?'
That is, after applying a logistic (or any regression) model that estimates
each customer's probability (or predicted dependent variable) to purchase,
they want to know if they should mail everyone on the database (No!)
or just some of them (Yes!). Which ones? Those that have the highest
propensity to respond? Probably, to a certain extent. And that extent is
financial. Lift charts show how a model is expected to perform, on average,
but then the financials hit and ROI comes into play, as it should.

Lift charts

A common and important tool, especially in direct/database marketing is the lift (or gain) chart. This is a simple analytic device to ascertain general fit as well as a targeting aid in terms of how deep to mail.

The general procedure is to run the logit model and output the probability to respond. Sort the database by probability to respond and divide into 10 (there's nothing especially magic about 10, it could be more or less) equal 'buckets'. Then count the number of actual responders in each decile. If the model is a good one, there will be a lot more responders in the upper deciles and a lot fewer responders in the lower deciles.

As an example, assume the average response rate is 1.9%. We have 60,000 total observations (customers). Each decile has 6,000 customers in it, some of them have responded and some of them have not. Overall there are 1,156 responders (1,156 / 60,000 = 1.9%). So, randomly, we would expect on average 115.5 in each decile. Instead, because the model works, there may be 400 (responders or events) in decile 1 and it decreases until the bottom decile has 0 responders in it.

The 'lift' is defined as the number of responders in each decile divided by the average (expected) number of responders. In decile 1 this means 400 / 115.5 = 348%. This shows us that the first decile has a lift of > 3X, that there are 3.48 times more responders there than average. It also says that those in the top decile who did not respond are very good targets, since again, they all 'look alike'. This is an indication the model can discriminate the responders from the non-responders.

Note that in each decile there are 6,000 customers. There are 400 who have already responded in decile 1. All of the customers in decile 1 have a high probability of top 10% responding. There are 5,400 more potential targets in decile 1 that have NOT responded. This is the place to focus targeting and this is why it's called 'clone modelling'.

To briefly address the database marketing question 'How deep do I mail?', let's look at the lift chart (Figure 10.1). This is an accumulation of actual responders compared to expected responders. Depending on budget, this lift chart helps to target. Most database marketers will mail as far as any decile out-responds the average. That is, until the lift is < 100%. Another way of saying this is to mail until the maximum distance between the curves is achieved. However, as a practical matter, most direct marketers (especially cataloguers) have a set budget and can only AFFORD to mail

FIGURE 10.1   Lift chart

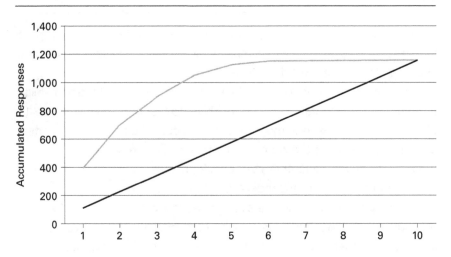

so deep, regardless of the statistical performance of the model. Thus, most of the attention is on the first few deciles.

Scoring the database with probability formula

Typically after a logistic regression is run, especially in a database marketing process, the model has to be applied to score the database. Yes, SAS now has 'proc score' but I want you to be able to do it yourself and to understand what's happening. It's old-fashioned but you will know more.

Take the model in Table 10.1 with probability to purchase. That is, the dependent variable is purchase = 1 for the event and purchase = 0 for the non-event. Because of the logistic curve bounding between 0 and 1, the formula for probability = $1 / (1 + e^{-Z})$ where $Z = \alpha + \beta X_i$. For the above model this means:

$$\text{Probability} = 1 / [1 + 2.71828 \wedge - (4.566 + X1 * -0.003 + X2 * 1.265 + X3 * 0.003)]$$

This returns a probability between 0 and 100% for each customer (2.71828 = e). So apply this formula to your database and each customer will have a score (that can be used for a lift chart) for probability to purchase.

The lift chart is based on the above probability formula.

TABLE 10.1 Probability: model output

INDEPENDENT VARIABLE	PARAMETER ESTIMATE
Intercept	4.566
X1	−0.003
X2	1.265
X3	0.003

Now look at Table 10.2. This shows the 1.9% expected response and the decile statistics. Again, the database is scored with each customer's probability to purchase and then SORTED from highest to lowest. This is then divided into 10 equal groups (deciles). Then the actual model responses are counted in each decile. Note that in decile 1 there are 6,000 customers and 400 actually responded. In decile 2 there are 6,000 customers and 300 actually responded, and so on. Note that in each

TABLE 10.2 Lift metrics

1.9%	N	modl resp	acc modl resp	exp resp	acc exp resp	lift
decile1	6,000	400	400	115	115	3.48
decile2	6,000	300	700	115	230	3.04
decile3	6,000	200	900	115	345	2.61
decile4	6,000	150	1,050	115	460	2.28
decile5	6,000	75	1,125	116	576	1.95
decile6	6,000	25	1,150	116	692	1.66
decile7	6,000	5	1,155	116	808	1.43
decile8	6,000	1	1,156	116	924	1.25
decile9	6,000	0	1,156	116	1,040	1.11
decile10	6,000	0	1,156	116	1,156	1.00
	60,000	1,156		1,156		

subsequent decile the number of responses decreases. This proves the model discriminates from those most likely to purchase down to those not likely to purchase. The next column C (acc modl resp) accumulates these responses so that in decile 2 there are an accumulated 400 + 300 for a total of 700 responses, and so on.

The next column is the expected responses. On average we expect 115.5 in each random decile. These are also accumulated and Figure 10.1 details these two columns. The lift is the model accumulation over the expected accumulation. In decile one this is 400 / 115 = 3.48. In decile 2 this is 700 / 230. See?

How deep to mail is usually a rule: 'stop at the decile where these two differences are greatest.' In this case it's decile 4: 1,050 − 460 = 590, which is the largest difference. But let's apply financials to that as well.

Table 10.3 shows how the rule works. Say the cost of mailing each piece is 0.75, so 6,000 * 0.75 = 4,500. If an average purchase is 50, so decile 1 model is 50 * 400 = 20,000 and for expected it is 50 * 115 = 5,750. So the net of the model in decile 1 is 20,000 − 4,500 = 15,500 and the

TABLE 10.3   How deep to mail

mail	cost/ mail	modl rev	expected	net modl	net exp	acc mdl rev	acc mdl exp	net rev
6,000	4,500	20,000	5,750	15,500	1,250	20,000	4,500	15,500
6,000	4,500	15,000	5,750	10,500	1,250	35,000	9,000	26,000
6,000	4,500	10,000	5,750	5,500	1,250	45,000	13,500	31,500
6,000	4,500	7,500	5,750	0	1,250	52,500	18,000	34,500
6,000	4,500	3,750	5,800	0	1,300	56,250	22,500	33,750
6,000	4,500	1,250	5,800	0	1,300	57,500	27,000	30,500
6,000	4,500	250	5,800	0	1,300	57,750	31,500	26,250
6,000	4,500	50	5,800	0	1,300	57,800	36,000	21,800
6,000	4,500	0	5,800	0	1,300	57,800	40,500	17,300
6,000	4,500	0	5,800	0	1,300	57,800	45,000	12,800
60,000	45,000	57,800	57,800	31,500	12,800			

random side is 5,750 – 4,500 = 1,250. Note the numbers in the box to the right of Table 10.3, showing the accumulated model revenue and expenses. We mail to decile 4 because it has the largest accumulated net revenue of 34,500. Mailing to any other decile would NOT bring in as much revenue. Comparing the ROI at this decile shows the model of 192%, 52,500 – 1,800) / 1,800 = 192% and the random of 28%.

Conclusion

Every analytic output should come with a financial implications scenario. There are financial implications whether you as the analyst show them or not – it can be guaranteed that your senior marketing audience is immediately thinking, 'Yes, and how much will this help me sell more stuff, what will it cost, what is the return?' Therefore, you should beat them to the punch and always include revenue potential, cost scenarios, risk/probability conditions, and other key factors.

One of the key ways to do this and demonstrate that the model works is via a lift chart. This is a simple table that arranges predicted probabilities from top to bottom and then sees if the model tended to predict more events in the high end (top deciles) than in the low end (lower deciles). Then these metrics can compare to random or average and a 'lift' is calculated. Lastly, the 'cost of being wrong' can be calculated by estimating mailing cost etc and finding the deepest and most efficient decile in which to mail.

Checklist

You'll be the smartest person in the room if you:

☐ Constantly demand a financial implication for every (especially direct mail) campaign.

☐ Remember a lift chart can be done for any type of regression, ordinary, logistic, Poisson, survival, etc.

☐ Always include a lift chart as: 1) a way to ascertain model fit; and 2) an indication of financial performance.

THE BENEFITS OF   11
PRODUCT BUNDLING

MARKETING QUESTION

How should products be bundled together? What is a market basket?

ANALYTIC SOLUTION

Logistic regression and predictive market basket analysis

In typical practice, market basket analysis (MBA) is a backward looking exercise. It uses descriptive procedures (frequencies, correlation, mathematical KPIs, etc) and outputs those products that tend to be purchased together. That's what descriptive techniques do: show what happened, explain how we got here, etc. That gives no insights into what marketers should do with that output. Descriptive analysis does not try to give a

WHY or suggest WHAT WE SHOULD DO, just displays past historical trends. The point of MBA is to understand which products are purchased together.

Predictive analytics, here using logistic regression, shows how much the probability of a product purchase increases/decreases given another product purchase. This gives marketers a strategic lever to use in bundling.

What is a market basket?

Backing up a little, let's get clear just what we're talking about. In economics, a market basket is a fixed collection of items that consumers buy. This is used for metrics such as CPI (inflation). In marketing, a market basket is any two or more items bought together.

Market basket analysis is used, especially in retail/consumer packaged goods (CPG), to bundle and offer promotions and gain insight in shopping/purchasing patterns. 'Market basket analysis' does not, by itself, describe HOW the analysis is done. That is, there is no associated technique with those words.

How is it usually done?

There are three general uses of data: descriptive, predictive and prescriptive. As previously mentioned, descriptive is about the past, predictive uses statistical analysis to calculate a change on an output variable (eg sales) given a change in an input variable (eg price) and prescriptive is a system that tries to optimize some metric (typically profit, satisfaction, etc). Descriptive data (means, frequencies, KPIs, etc) is a necessary, but not usually sufficient, step. Always get to at least the predictive step as soon as possible.

(Note again that predictive here does not mean forecasted. That is, predicted here does not mean thrusting into the future. Structural analysis uses models to simulate the market, and estimate (predict) what causes what to happen. That is, using regression, a change in price shows an estimated (predicted) change in revenue. By 'predicted' we mean an estimate of some (typically dependent) variable given some change in an input variable.)

Market basket analysis often uses descriptive techniques. Sometimes it is just a 'report' of what percentage of items are purchased together. Think of correlation analysis, which shows strength and direction, and NOT causality.

Affinity analysis (a slight step above) is mathematical, not statistical. Affinity analysis (association rules etc) simply calculates the percentage of time combinations of products that are purchased together. Obviously there is no probability involved. It is concerned with the rate of products purchased together, and not with a distribution around that association. It provides no control for other variables interacting (seasonality, marcomm, etc). It provides no diagnostics of fit. While it is very common and very useful, it is NOT predictive – therefore NOT so actionable.

Logistic regression

Let's talk again about logistic regression. This is an ancient and well-known statistical technique, probably the analytic pillar upon which database marketing has been built. It is similar to ordinary regression in that there is a dependent variable that depends on one or more independent variables. There is a coefficient (although interpretation is not the same) and there is a (type of) t-test around each independent variable for significance.

The differences are that the dependent variable is binary (having two values, 0 or 1) in logistic and continuous in ordinary regression and to interpret the coefficients requires exponentiation. Because the dependent variable is binary, the result is heteroscedasticity. There is no (real) R^2, and 'fit' is about classification.

How to estimate/predict the market basket

The use of logistic regression in terms of market basket becomes obvious when it is understood that the predicted dependent variable is a probability. The formula to estimate probability from logistic regression is:

$$P_{(i)} = 1 / 1 + e^{-Z}$$

where $Z = \alpha + \beta X_i$. This means that the independent variables can be products purchased in a market basket to predict likelihood to purchase another product as the dependent variable. The above means to specifically take each (major) category of product (focus driven by strategy) and running a separate model for each, putting in all significant other products as independent variables. For example, say we have only three products, x, y and z. The idea is to design three models and test the significance of each, meaning using logistic regression:

$$x = f(y,z)$$
$$y = f(x,z)$$
$$z = f(x,y).$$

Of course other variables (marcomm, season, etc) can go into the model as appropriate but the interest is whether or not the independent (product) variables are significant in predicting (and to what extent) the probability of purchasing the dependent product. Of course, after significance is achieved, the insights generated are around the sign of the independent variable, ie does the independent product increase or decrease the probability of purchasing the dependent product.

Business case

Scott met with his team on Monday morning to discuss an interesting question posed by the marketing department.

'Which products go together?' Scott asked. 'Which of our categories should be bundled and messaged together, and which should not?'

The group nodded in anticipation of another analytic challenge.

'It's expensive and irrelevant to try to promote every product to every prospect or customer. Targeting is about who is likely to buy different combinations of major product categories.'

'You mean a market basket.'

'That's right,' said Scott.

'We did a market basket a couple of years ago but it went nowhere,' Mark said. 'The testing was not effective.'

'Really? Becky thought this was a new idea for us.'

'Well, it was a while back but regarded as not offering strategies.'

'I see. Who led that effort?'

'Your predecessor. We did correlations between all product categories and it mostly made sense to us. When we showed it to marketing strategy and marcomm they did not know what to do with it. They put together a few A/B tests and most of the results were not conclusive or the lift was not dramatic. I can see if I can dig it up if you like.'

'Great. I'd like us to think about a modelling approach. That is, predictive rather than what sounds like something descriptive as done before. Let's investigate using logit.'

Scott went through some simple PowerPoint overviews.

'So, say we do a series of models, by each major product category. That is, consumer electronics = f(women's accessories, jewellery and watches, furniture, entertainment, etc).

'This means each row is an individual model. The independent variables are binary, coded as a 1 if the customer bought that category and a 0 if not. Table 11.1 details the output for all of the models. Note that other independent variables can be included in the model, if significant. These would often be seasonality, consumer confidence, promotions sent, etc.

'To interpret, look at the home décor model. If a customer bought consumer electronics, that increases the probability of buying home décor by 29 per cent. If a customer bought newborn/infant items, that decreases the probability of buying home décor by 37 per cent. If a customer bought furniture, that increases the probability of buying home décor by 121 per cent.

'This has implications especially for bundling and messaging. That is, offering home décor and furniture together makes great sense, but offering home décor and newborn/infant items does not make sense.'

Everyone smiled and seemed excited by the possibility.

Scott continued. 'Here is a special note about products purchased together. If it is known, via above, that home décor and furniture tend to go together, these can be and should be bundled together, messaged together, etc. But there is no reason to PROMOTE them together, to discount them together because they are purchased together anyway. This is part of insights we give to strategy.'

So Scott's team developed the models and presented the results to senior management. Most of the questions had to do with the difference between correlation and logistic regression.

'A couple of key things,' Scott said. 'Correlation is descriptive and tells two things: strength and direction. It is bounded from –100% to + 100%. There are no diagnostics and it does not control for anything else except those two variables and it gives you no actionability, no levers to pull. Logistic regression is predictive, it is a statistical model that controls for any and all other independent variables we have, including price changes,

TABLE 11.1 Market basket modelling with logistic regression

	CONSUMER ELECTRON	WOMEN'S ACCESSOR	NEWBORN, INFANT, ETC.	JEWELRY, WATCHES	FURNITURE	HOME DÉCOR	ENTERTAIN	SPORTING GOODS
CONSUMER ELECTRON	XXX	Insig	Insig	−23%	34%	26%	98%	12%
WOMEN'S ACCESSOR	Insig	XXX	39%	68%	22%	21%	Insig	−31%
NEWBORN, INFANT, ETC.	Insig	43%	XXX	−11%	−21%	−31%	29%	−34%
JEWELLERY, WATCHES	−29%	71%	−22%	XXX	12%	24%	−11%	−34%
FURNITURE	31%	18%	−17%	9%	XXX	115%	37%	29%
HOME DÉCOR	29%	24%	−37%	21%	121%	XXX	31%	12%
ENTERTAIN	85%	Insig	31%	−9%	41%	29%	XXX	31%
SPORTING GOODS	18%	−37%	−29%	−29%	24%	9%	33%	XXX

seasonality, marcomm, etc. Primarily it gives you decisions to make. You can see how the purchase of one product increases or decreases the probability of purchasing another product. This has implications for messaging and bundling, both those products that go together and strategies for those that do NOT go together.'

The senior leadership team seemed to understand and the presentation was successful. They started talking about implementation plans. Scott smiled.

Conclusion

Logistic regression is a pivotal analytic technique especially in marketing analytics. This is because much of consumer behaviour is choice behaviour and many choices are binary.

The market basket analysis advocated here is a predictive, rather than a descriptive technique. The motto is: If given a choice, always go beyond mere descriptive techniques and apply predictive techniques. In this case logistic regression was used as a predictive analytic tool to quantify how purchasing one product increases or decreases the probability of buying another product. This is far more insightful for marketers than descriptive (association rules, affinity analysis, etc) techniques.

Checklist

You'll be the smartest person in the room if you:

☐   Remember that logistic regression is more complicated than ordinary regression but offers intriguing insights for marketers, especially in terms of customer choice behaviour.

☐   Point out the differences in descriptive (association rules and affinity) vs. predictive market basket analysis (MBA).

☐   Always advocate a predictive level of analysis whenever possible; that is, do not settle for descriptive analysis.

ESTIMATING TIME OF PURCHASE

12

MARKETING QUESTION

When are my customers most likely to buy?

ANALYTIC SOLUTION

Survival analysis

Introduction

Survival analysis is an especially interesting and powerful technique. In terms of marketing science it is relativity new, mostly getting exposure in the last 20 years or so. It answers a very important and particular question: 'WHEN is an event (eg purchase, response, churn) most likely to occur?' I'd submit this is a more relevant question than: 'How likely is an event (purchase, response, churn) to occur?' That is, a customer may be VERY likely to purchase but not for 10 months. Is timing information of value? Of course it is; time is money.

Beware though. Given the increase in actionable information, it should be no surprise that survival analysis is more complex than logistic regression. Remember how much more complex logistic regression was than ordinary regression?

Conceptual overview of survival analysis

Survival analysis (via proportional hazards modelling) was essentially invented by Sir David Cox in 1972 with his seminal and oft-quoted paper, 'Regression Models and Life Tables' in the *Journal of the Royal Statistical Society*. It's important to note this technique was specifically designed to study time-until-event problems. This came out of bio-statistics and the event of study was typically death. That's why it's called 'survival analysis'.

The general use case was in drug treatment. For example, a drug study would divide a panel into two groups, one group got the new drug and the other group did not. Every month the test subjects were called and basically asked, 'Are you still alive?' and their survival was tracked. There would be two curves developed, one following the treatment group and another following the non-treatment group. If the treatment tended to work, the time until the event (death) was increased.

One major issue involved censored observations. It's an easy matter to compare the average survival times of the treatment vs. the non-treatment group. But what about those subjects who dropped out of the study because they moved away or lost contact? Or the study ended and not everyone had yet died? Each of these involves censored observations. The question about what to do with these kinds of observations is why Cox regression was created, a non-parametric partial likelihood technique, which he called proportional hazards. It deals with censored observations, which are those patients that have an unknown time-until-event status. This unknown time until event can be caused by either not having the event at the time of the analysis or their contact was lost.

What about those subjects who died from another cause and not the cause the test drug was treating? Are there other variables (covariates) that influence (increase or decrease) the time until the event? These questions involve extensions of the general survival model. The first is about competing risks and the second is about regression involving independent variables. These will be dealt with soon enough.

More about survival analysis

As mentioned above, survival analysis came from bio-statistics in the early 1970s where the subject studied was an event – death. Survival analysis is about modelling the time until an event. In bio-statistics the event is typically death but in marketing the event can be response, purchase, churn, etc.

Due to the nature of survival studies, there are a couple of characteristics that are endemic to this technique. As alluded to earlier, the dependent variable is time until an event, so time is built into the analysis. The second endemic thing to survival analysis is observations that are censored. A censored observation is either an observation that has not had the event or an observation that was lost to the study and there is no knowledge of having the event or not – but we do know at some point in time that observation has not had the event.

In marketing it is common for the event to be a purchase. Imagine scoring a database of customers with time until purchase. That is far more actionable than, from logistic regression, probability of purchase.

Let's talk about censored observations. What can be done about them? Remember these are observations whose outcomes we do not know. We could delete them. That would be simple but depending how many there are that might mean throwing away a lot of data. Also, they might be the most interesting data of all, so deleting them is probably a bad idea. (Never delete observations. It's an 'Off with their heads!' crime.) We could just give the max time until an event to all those that have not had the event. This would also be a bad idea, especially if a large portion of the sample is censored, as is often the case. (It can be shown that throwing away a lot of censored data will bias any results.) Thus, we need a technique that can deal with censored data. Also, deleting censored observations ignore a lot of information. While we don't know when (or even if) the customer purchased, we do know that, as of a certain time, they did NOT purchase. So we have part of their curve, part of their information, part of their behaviour. This should never be deleted. This is why Cox invented partial likelihood.

FIGURE 12.1   Survival curve

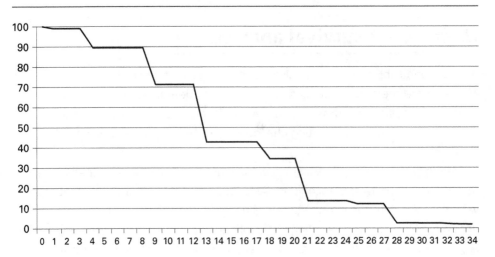

Figure 12.1 is a general survival curve. The vertical axis is a count of those in the 'risk set' and it starts out with 100 per cent. That is, at time 0 everyone is 'at risk' of having the event and no one has had the event. At Day 1, that is, after one day, 1 person died (had the event) and there are now 99 that are left at risk. No one died for three days until 9 had the event at Day 5, and so on. Note that at about Day 12, 25 had the event.

Now note Figure 12.2. One survival curve is the same as that in Figure 12.1, but the other one is 'further out'. Note that 50 per cent of the first curve is reached at 14 days, but the second curve does not reach 50 per cent until 28 days. That is, they 'live longer'.

Survival analysis is a type of regression, but with a twist. It does not use maximum likelihood, but partial likelihood. (The most common form of survival analysis, proportional hazards, uses partial likelihood.) The dependent variable has now two parts: time until the event and whether the event has occurred or not. This allows using the censored observations.

Figure 12.2 illustrates survival graphs showing different treatments. Note that 50 per cent remain on one curve at about 14 days. The second curve shows a different treatment that moves out 50 per cent to about 29 days. This can be key for marketing.

FIGURE 12.2 Survival curves with different treatments

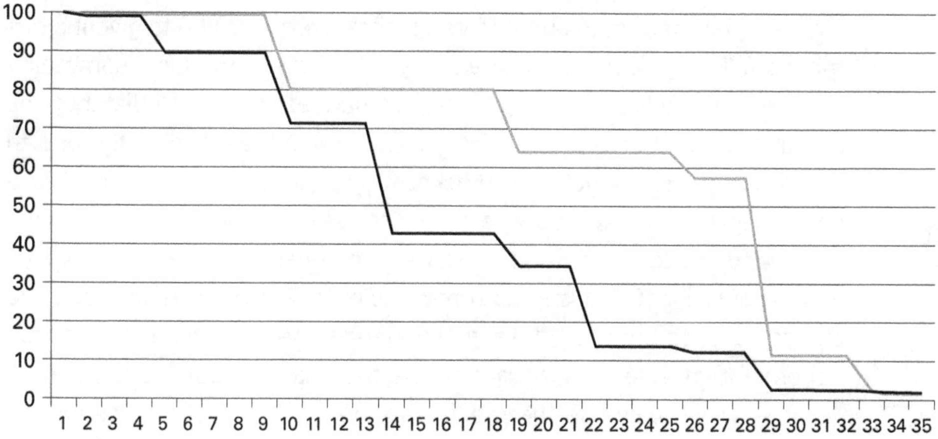

Much of Cox regression is not about the survival curve, but the hazard rate. The hazard is nearly the reciprocal of the survival curve. This ends up as the instantaneous risk that an event will occur at some particular time. Think of metrics like miles per hour as analogous to the hazard rate. At 40 miles per hour you will travel 40 miles in one hour if speed remains the same. The hazard quantifies the rate of the event in each period of time.

SAS does both survival modelling (with proc lifereg) and hazard modelling (as proc phreg). SPSS only does hazard modelling (as Cox regression). Lifereg does left and interval censoring while phreg does only right censoring. (This is not usually an issue for marketing.) With lifereg a distribution must be specified, but with phreg (as it's semi-parametric) there is no distribution. This is one of the advantages of phreg. The other advantage is that it can incorporate time-varying independent variables (eg income that changes over time), while lifereg does not. This is not usually much of an issue for marketing.

I typically use lifereg as it easily outputs a time-until-event prediction, it is on the survival curve and is relatively easy to understand and interpret. That's what we'll demonstrate here.

I might mention that survival analysis is not just about the time-until-event prediction. As with all regressions the independent variables are strategic levers. Say we find that for every 1,000 e-mails we send, purchases tend to happen three days sooner. Do you see the financial implications here? How valuable is it to know you have incentivized a group of customers to making purchases earlier? If this does not interest you then you are in the wrong career field.

A procedure suggestion and pseudo-fit

First, an important note about lifereg is that it requires you to give it a distribution. (Phreg does not require that you give it a distribution, something a lot of analysts like.) In using lifereg, I'd suggest testing all distributions and the one that fits the best (lowest BIC or log likelihood) is the one to use. Another view would be to acknowledge that the distribution has a shape and ascertain what shape makes sense given the data you're using.

Second, while R^2 as a metric makes no sense (same as with logistic regression) a lot of analysts like some kind of R^2. To review, R^2 in OLS is the shared variance between the actual dependent variable and the predicted dependent variable. In survival analysis there is no predicted dependent variable. Most folks use the median as the prediction and that's OK. I'd suggest running a simple model with, and without, covariates. That is, in SAS with proc lifereg, run the model without the covariates (independent variables) and collect the –2 log likelihood stat. Then run the model with the covariates and collect the –2LL stat and divide. This metric (by analogy) shows the percentage of explained over the total likelihood.

Business case

Scott called his team together.

'I'd like us to start thinking about a new, or at least an added technique to use in our database targeting. At my last job I asked marketers what they really needed to know in order to do their job and it came out that if they knew WHEN a customer was going to purchase a certain product they would concentrate all their efforts just before that time. That is, if someone were going to purchase a TV in nine months, around Month 8 we would send them a catalogue about that product.'

'Isn't that just a logistic regression? Probability to buy at a certain time? I mean, can't we do a model for January and another model for February, etc?'

'It is probably NOT a logistic regression. Logit assumes independence of events. That is, the probability to buy in March is NOT independent, but dependent on the customer NOT buying in February and NOT buying in January, see? It is not an equal choice but a dependent choice.'

'Oh yes, I see. So what then?'

'We did survival analysis,' Scott smiled.

'Not sure what that is.'

'It's a technique designed for time-until-event analysis. It's called survival analysis because it came out of bio-stats and they studied time until death.'

'Oh.'

'Yes. It gives us a way to predict when a purchase will happen. The most powerful thing is that it'll give us a prediction even of those that HAVE NOT PURCHASED YET.'

'How can that be?'

'It uses partial likelihood (in the case of proportional hazards, anyway) and calls these censored observations. We'll model the survival curve though but the point is the same. We can get a prediction of when a purchase will happen next.'

'That is amazing. We would create a list of customers with a most likely time to purchase each product?'

Scott rubbed his chin. 'Yes. It's a prediction of when each customer is going to purchase. Imagine having the database scored with number of days until each customer is likely to buy.'

They all sat there, thinking, smiling.

'We'd just sort the database by those more likely to buy sooner and they would get the communication.'

Scott nodded.

(It's important to make a clarification about a trap a lot of people fall into. Survival analysis is a technique specifically designed to estimate and understand time-until-event problems. The underlying assumption is that each time period is independent of each other time period. That is, the prediction has no 'memory'. Some under-educated/under-experienced analysts think that if we are, say, trying to predict what month an event will happen (January, February, etc) they can do 12 logits and have one model for January, another for February, and so on. The collected data would have a 1 if the customer purchased in January and a 0 if not; likewise, if the model was for February a customer would have a 1 if they purchased in February and a 0 if not. This seems like it would work, right? Wrong. February is not independent of January. In order for the customer to buy in February they had to decide NOT to buy in January. This is why logit is inappropriate.)

'Let me also make a suggestion,' Scott continued, 'about modelling survival curves. In ordinary regression the assumption of a normal distribution for the error term is common. But since survival modelling has a dependent variable as ln(Time) there are (in SAS) other possibilities. The distribution of the error term generates a corresponding distribution for time.'

'What does that mean for us as we're running the model?'

'Well it means that you have to make a choice, an assumption, as to the distribution of time, which you don't really know. My suggestion is to test all five distributions and use the one that fits the best. The five choices are Weibull, exponential, gamma, log-logistic and log-normal.'

'How do we know which fits the best?'

'SAS outputs both −LL and AIC. LL = log likelihood and AIC = Akaike Information Criteria. They both basically use the likelihood function and the minimum value is the best fit. That is, run the model with all five distributions and the one closest to (of −LL and/or AIC) is the "best" model. Use THAT distribution.'

'Easy enough. We'll show you what we come up with.'

And off they went.

Model output and interpretation

So Scott's team investigated survival analysis and concluded it was worth a shot. It seemed to give a way to answer the key question, 'WHEN is a customer most likely to purchase?'

Table 12.1 lists the final purchase model using lifereg. The variables are all significant at the 95% level. The first column is the name of the independent variable. The interpretation of lifereg coefficients requires transformations. This gets the parameter estimates into a form to make strategic interpretation.

The next column is the beta coefficient. This is what SAS outputs but, as with logistic regression, is not very meaningful. A negative coefficient tends to bring the event of a purchase in; a positive coefficient tends to push the event (purchase) out. This is a regression output so in that regard interpretation is the same, *ceteris paribus*.

To get percentage impacts on time until event (TTE), each beta coefficient must be exponentiated, e^B. That's the third column. The next column subtracts 1 from it and converts it into a percentage. Note that, for example, RECENT ONLINE VISIT e^Beta is a 0.987 impact on time, or, if 1 is subtracted shows a 1.3% decrease in average TTE. To convert that to a time scale – say the average is 11 weeks – this means −0.013 * 11 = −0.148 weeks. The interpretation is that if a customer had a recent online visit that tends to pull in (shorten) TTE by 0.148 weeks. Not very impactful, but it makes sense.

TABLE 12.1 Survival analysis: interpreting model output

INDEPENDENT VARIABLES	Beta	e^B	(e^B)-1	AVG TTE
ANY PREVIOUS PURCH	−0.001	0.999	−0.001	−0.012
RECENT ONLINE VISIT	−0.014	0.987	−0.013	−0.148
# DIRECT MAILS	0.157	1.17	0.17	1.865
# E-MAILS OPENED	−0.011	0.989	−0.011	−0.12
# E-MAILS CLICKED	−0.033	0.968	−0.032	−0.352
INCOME	−0.051	0.95	−0.05	−0.547
SIZE HOUSEHOLD	−0.038	0.963	−0.037	−0.408
EDUCATION	−0.023	0.977	−0.023	−0.249
BLUE COLLAR OCCUPAT	0.151	1.163	0.163	1.792
# PROMOTIONS SENT	−0.006	0.994	−0.006	−0.066
PURCH LESS THAN MONTH	2.09	8.085	7.085	77.934

Notice the last variable, PURCH LESS THAN MONTH. See how it's positive, 2.09? This means if the customer has purchased in the last month the time until (another) purchase is pushed out by ((e^B)-1) * 11 = 77.934 weeks. See how this works? See how strategically insightful survival analysis can be? You can build a business case around marcomm sent (cost of marcomm) and decreasing the time until purchase (revenue realized sooner).

As typically used on a database, each customer is scored with time until the event, in this case, time until a purchase. The database is sorted and a list is designed with those most likely to purchase next (see Table 12.2). This time until event (TTE) is at the (50% decile) median.

Note that customer 1,000 is expected to purchase in 3.3 weeks and customer 1,030 is expected to purchase in 14.9 weeks. Using survival analysis (in SAS, proc lifereg) allowed Scott's team to score the database with those likely to purchase sooner. This list is more actionable than using logistic regression, where the score is just probability to purchase.

TABLE 12.2   Predicted time until event

CUSTOMER ID	TTE
1000	3.365
1002	3.702
1004	4.072
1006	4.479
1011	5.151
1013	5.923
1015	6.812
1017	7.834
1022	9.009
1024	10.36
1026	12.43
1030	14.92

Conclusion

Survival analysis is not a common topic in marketing analytics but it should be. While it's true that marketers and bio-statisticians (where survival analysis originated) do not move in the same circles, I've now given you some of the basics, so it's 'time' to get to work.

Checklist

You'll be the smartest person in the room if you:

☐ Point out that 'time until an event' is a more relevant marketing question than 'probability of an event'.

☐ Remember that survival analysis came out of bio-statistics and is somewhat rare in marketing, but very powerful.

☐ Observe that there are two 'flavours' of survival analysis: lifereg and proportional hazards. Lifereg models the survival curve and proportional hazards models the hazard rate.

☐ Champion competing risks, a natural output of survival analysis. In marketing, this gives time until various events or time until multiple products purchased.

☐ Understand that predictive lifetime value (using survival analysis) is more insightful than descriptive lifetime value.

INVESTIGATING THE 13
TIME OF PRODUCT
PURCHASE

MARKETING QUESTION

Which products are my customers most likely to buy next? In what order?

ANALYTIC SOLUTION

Survival analysis using competing risks

Now let's talk about competing risks. While survival analysis is about death, the study usually is interested in ONE kind of death, or death from ONE cause. For example, the bio-stat study is about death by heart attack and not about death by cancer or death by a car accident. But it's true that in a study of death by heart attack a patient is also at risk for other kinds of death. This is called competing risks.

Competing risks

In the marketing arena, while the focus might be on a purchase event for TVs, the customer is also 'at risk' for purchasing other things, like a pair of shoes or a bottle of wine. The very powerful thing this will give is not just time until a purchase, but WHICH product is most likely to be purchased next; ie in what order?

Fortunately, this is an easy job of just coding the events of interest. Scott can code for an event as TV purchase, all else coded as a non-event. He can do another model as a purchase event of, say, shoes, all else is a non-event; that is, all other things are censored. Table 13.1 shows three models, a purchase event for TV, shoes and wine.

Let's look at the model for TV purchase. Some customers have purchased a TV and some have not. Those who have not purchased a TV are coded as a censored observation. Then the model is run with appropriate independent variables, eg price, marcomm and seasonality, and the resulting output will show time until purchase of a TV, for EVERYONE: those that have already purchased and those that have not.

Another model will be designed for shoe purchases. Those who have purchased shoes had the event and those who have not purchased shoes are censored. Note that time until event is coded as the time until a shoe purchase. And the resulting model shows estimated time until purchase of shoes. The entire database can be coded as such.

An obvious question is: how deep into product hierarchy (SKUs) should a model be run? Always think about modelling from the consumer's point of view, NOT the firm's point of view. Marketing analytics is all about understanding and incentivizing and changing consumer behaviour. So the question is not how many SKUs does the firm have, but which levels of a product hierarchy does a consumer view as a different product. In the case of jeans, the firm can sell cuffed jeans, different decorations on jeans, different washes, etc. They are ALL jeans. Does the consumer actually see dark washed jeans as a different product to stone-washed jeans? If the answer is yes, then the model should be at that level. If the answer is 'jeans are jeans' then the model should be at that level. I myself would argue that a pair of jeans is a pair of jeans. That is, do the analysis at the higher level of a product's hierarchy.

TABLE 13.1   Database scored with time-until-product purchase

CUSTOMER ID	TT TV PURCH	TT shoe PURCH	TT wine PURCH
1000	3.365	75.66	39.51
1002	3.702	88.2	45.95
1004	4.072	111.2	55.66
1006	4.479	15.05	19.66
1011	5.151	13.07	9.109
1013	5.923	9.945	7.934
1015	6.812	22.24	144.5
1017	7.834	3.011	5.422
1022	9.009	2.613	5.811
1024	10.36	1.989	6.174
1026	12.43	4.448	8.44
1030	14.92	0.602	7.76

Conclusion

Competing risks is a powerful but little used marketing analytic technique. This is a way to predict what product each customer will buy in what order. This can be updated every month and the database scored with targeted products.

Checklist

You'll be the smartest person in the room if you:

☐ Suggest completing risks as an analytic technique to estimate each customer's next product to be purchased.

☐ Advocate a way to build an ROI based on estimated products purchased.

INCREASING CUSTOMER LIFETIME VALUE

14

MARKETING QUESTION

How do I estimate customer lifetime value? How do I know what increases value? How can I increase the value of a lower-tiered customer?

ANALYTIC SOLUTION

Survival and tobit analysis

Typically, lifetime value (LTV) is but a calculation using historical data. This calculation makes some rather heroic assumptions to project into the future but gives no insights into why a customer is lower valued, or how to make a customer higher valued. Using predictive techniques, here survival analysis, gives an indication into what causes purchases to happen sooner, and thus how to increase LTV.

Descriptive analysis

Lifetime value is typically just done as a calculation, using past (historical) data. That is, it's only descriptive.

While there are many versions of LTV (depending on data, industry, interest, etc) the following is conceptually applied to all. LTV, via descriptive analysis:

1 Uses historical data to sum up each customer's total revenue.

2 This sum then has subtracted from it some costs: typically cost to serve, cost to market, cost of goods sold, etc.

3 This net revenue is then converted into an annual average amount and depicted as a cash flow.

4 These cash flows are assumed to continue into the future and diminish over time (depending on durability, sales cycle, etc), often decreasing arbitrarily by, say, 10 per cent each year until they are effectively zero.

5 These (future, diminished) cash flows are then summed up and discounted (usually by weighted average cost of capital) to get their net present value (NPV).

6 This NPV is called LTV. This calculation is applied to each customer.

Thus, each customer has a value associated with it. The typical use is for marketers to find the 'high-valued' customers (based on past purchases). These high-valued customers get most of the communications, promotions/ discounts, marketing efforts, etc. Descriptive analysis is merely about targeting those already engaged (much like RFM).

This seems to be a good starting point but, as is usual with descriptive analysis, contributes nothing informative. Why is one customer more valuable, and will they continue to be? Is it possible to extract additional value, but at what cost? Is it possible to garner more revenue from a lower-valued customer because they are more loyal or cost less to serve? What part of the marketing mix is each customer most sensitive to?

LTV (as described above) gives no implications for strategy. The only strategy is to offer and promote to (only) the high-valued customers.

Predictive analysis

How would LTV change using predictive analysis instead of descriptive analysis? First, note that while LTV is a future-oriented metric, descriptive analysis uses historical (past) data and the entire metric is built on that, with assumptions about the future applied unilaterally to every customer. Predictive analysis specifically thrusts LTV into the future (where it belongs) by using independent variables to predict the next time until purchase. Since the major customer behaviour driving LTV is timing, amount and number of purchases, a statistical technique needs to be used that predicts time until an event. (Ordinary regression predicting the LTV amount ignores timing and number of purchases.)

Survival analysis is a technique designed specifically to study time until event problems. It has timing built into it and thus a future view is already embedded in the algorithm. This removes much of the arbitrariness of typical (descriptive) LTV calculations.

The advantage of survival modelling is that it takes into account ALL customers' behaviour, whether they purchased or not. Just to make an obvious point, if OLS was used to predict when a particular product was purchased, typically a large percentage of customers have not made that purchase. Say product X has a 10 per cent purchase rate, meaning that 90 per cent of customers have not made that purchase. Using ordinary regression begs the question: what do you do with those that have not had the event, those that have NOT purchased? A couple of choices present themselves, both bad. One possibility is to ignore those that did not purchase and model the time until purchase using ONLY those that did purchase. This means you throw away 90 per cent of the customers and those 90 per cent are probably the most interesting observations because you are trying to get them to buy. The other common option is to give all those that did not purchase (90 per cent of them) the same value, typically, the longest time available. This means that 90 per cent of the file will have the very largest time until purchase, clearly not representative of the behaviour of customers. But with survival modelling, censored observations (those that did not have the event) are explicitly included.

So, what about using survival analysis to see which independent variables bring in a purchase? Decreasing time until purchase tends to increase LTV. While survival analysis can predict the next time until purchase, the strategic value of survival analysis is in using the independent variables to CHANGE the timing of purchases. That is, descriptive analysis shows what happened; predictive analysis gives a glimpse of what might CHANGE the future.

Strategy using LTV dictates understanding the causes of customer value: why a customer purchases, what increases/decreases the time until purchase, probability of purchasing at future times, etc. Then, when these insights are learned, marketing levers (shown as independent variables) are exploited to extract additional value from each customer. This means knowing that one customer is sensitive to price and that a discount will tend to decrease their time until purchase. That is, they will purchase sooner (maybe purchase larger total amounts and maybe purchase more often) with a discount. Another customer may prefer product X and product Y bundled together to increase the probability of purchase and this bundling decreases their time until purchase. This insight allows different strategies for different customer needs and sensitivities. Survival analysis applied to each customer yields insights to understand and incentivize changes in behaviour.

This means that just assuming the past behaviour will continue into the future (as descriptive analysis does), with no idea why, is no longer necessary. It's possible for descriptive and predictive analysis to give contradictory answers. Which is why 'crawling' might be detrimental to 'walking'.

If a firm can get a customer to purchase sooner, there is an increased chance of adding purchases – depending on the product. But even if the number of purchases is not increased, the firm getting revenue sooner will add to their financial value (time is money).

Also, a business case can be created by showing the trade-off in, for example, giving up margin but obtaining revenue faster. This means strategy can revolve around maximization of cost balanced against customer value.

The idea is to model next time until purchase, the baseline, and see how to improve that. How is this carried out? A behaviourally-based method would be to segment the customers (based on behaviour) and apply a survival model to each segment and score each individual customer. By behaviour is typically meant purchasing (amount, timing, share of products, etc) metrics and marcomm (open and click, direct mail coupons, etc) responses.

Introduction to tobit analysis

Tobit (after James Tobin, 1958) is a very interesting and powerful (although not commonly used) analytic technique, especially for marketing. The idea again is around censored observations, that is, the dependent variable is 'cut off' and truncated and replaced with (typically) zero or some maximum amount. The common example is a stadium that sells out for a concert. To estimate the demand for the concert requires an analytic choice: ordinary regression can be used but those who wanted to buy a seat could not get one, so the demand is truncated (eg made to be the maximum capacity) when in fact if the stadium were larger more seats would be sold. That is to say that if there were 10 per cent more people wanted a ticket than could not get one, the demand for those 10 per cent is replaced with the maximum rather than the true (greater than the maximum) amount. This means the distribution is truncated, artificially cut off.

In a marketing context, typically focussed on purchase, the idea is to predict the amount of purchase when there was none. Very similar to survival modelling (see Chapter 13), tobit will estimate the zero purchase amount with something higher than zero, based on the independent variables used.

Again let me point out that the common choice, OLS, is not a good choice. Ordinary regression will estimate purchase amount, but what if the product is not purchased very often? What will you do with those that did not purchase – their purchase amount is zero. Will you delete them? It is actually those very customers that are probably of most interest to you: how do you get them to purchase? So tobit, like survival modelling, gives a way to account for those that have not had the event, that is, censored observations, and provides an estimate for them.

Tobit creates a distribution that is part discrete and part continuous. It uses a transformed dependent variable that includes the censored observations (those that did not purchase). In essence it is a combination of probit (a binary variable technique similar to logistic regression but using the normal distribution rather than the logistic distribution) and ordinary regression; hence the name tobit (from Tobin and probit – who says statisticians have no sense of humour?)

FIGURE 14.1   Tobit conceptual framework

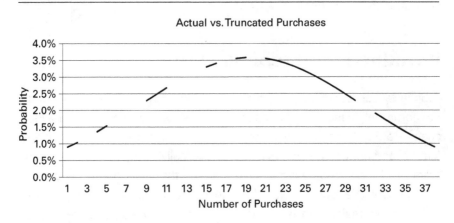

Figure 14.1 shows a distribution of purchases and non-purchases. The gaps in the distribution are the non-purchases, placed in the value based on a (contrived) tobit model. That is, the missing purchases are calculated by the equation resulting from the independent variables.

The obvious value is that, like survival modelling, we do not need to discard those that did not purchase, indeed we can estimate the amount of purchases they (should) have made. In SAS I usually use PROC GLIM. Say the dependent variable is purchamt and if a customer did not purchase they get a 0 for censored (0 = lower bound). Say there are three independent variables (x1, x2 and x3), the code would be:

```
    proc qlim data = LOCATION.NAME;
  model purchamt = x1 x2 x3;
  endogenous purchamt ~ censored(lb=0);
    output out = prob predicted prob proball; run;
```

Business case

Scott was up to his neck. He also had a project at work that was important and had a short deadline. Mark was in his office when he arrived.

'So have we ever done LTV before?'

'Sure,' Mark said. 'It was not used much but we calculated LTV for a couple of years.'

'How did you do it? You said you calculated LTV?'

'Yes, we added up the total past revenue per transaction and got a cash flow by average number of transactions. We assumed that same cash flow over the next 24 months and decreased the amount each time by I think 20 per cent. We put that into present value by discounting at some rate.'

'Yep, I've seen that done before.'

'Marketers said that targeting the highest-valued customers gave no difference than usual selections, RFM, etc. And they ignored the lower-valued customers.'

'Because they did not know what CAUSED the lower-valued customers to be lower valued. Or even the higher-valued customers to be higher valued. They had no insights, just past trends.'

'Yes, they had no causality, they could not predict changes...'

'They did not know which levers to pull.'

They were both laughing. 'Wow, such expertise!' said Mark.

'Well, let's see if we can improve on that. What is the first thing you'd change?'

Mark mused. 'Hmmmm. I would want it to be actionable.'

'Yes, right on. How?'

'Can it be done as a predictive model? Like we used logistic regression for market basket instead of correlation and affinity analysis. That is, instead of descriptive approaches, can it be a predictive technique?'

'I like it. What would you predict?'

'When will a purchase happen? How much the purchase is?'

'Sounds right. How about what product is purchased?'

'Sure, but it's getting complicated.'

Scott laughed. 'Yes, consumer behaviour IS complicated.'

So they both sat there a minute, musing. Then Scott said, 'As usual let's do segmentation first and try to design each segment with behaviours that hypothetically drive value. This would be transactions and marcomm, and if we have it, marketing research on satisfaction, competitive density, etc.'

Mark took notes.

'Then we will do a separate model on each segment on each major product category.'

Mark looked up and gulped.

Scott continued. 'The hard part is to get the data-set arranged to do that. We will need a separate data-set for each purchase event. Let's assume we're doing consumer electronics first. Put together a data-set of all those that purchased consumer electronics over the last three years. Many have not purchased at all, some purchased once, some purchased twice, etc.'

Scott drew Table 14.1 on the white board. 'Say we have those that did not purchase and those that purchased one time. TTE is time until event (a purchase event). What this data-set will do is to predict when those who did not purchase will make their first purchase.'

'I see,' Mark said. 'Then those who did purchase one time will be in a data-set with those who purchased twice. Then we will predict when

TABLE 14.1   Data-set and predicted first purchase

CUSTOMER	NUM_PURCH	TTE
1000	0	.
1002	0	.
1003	0	.
1005	1	39
1007	1	48
1009	0	.
1011	0	.
1013	1	44
1015	1	37
1019	1	29
1021	1	25
1023	0	.
1025	0	.
1030	0	.
1032	1	54
1034	1	76

TABLE 14.2   Data-set and predicted second purchase

CUSTOMER	NUM_PURCH	TTE
952	2	44
954	2	45
956	2	13
958	1	.
960	1	.
962	1	.
964	2	12
966	2	16
968	1	.
977	1	.
979	1	.
981	1	.
983	2	66
1004	2	54
1005	1	.
1009	2	2

those who purchased one time will purchase next, which will be their second time?'

Mark drew Table 14.2.

'That's right. Note your customer # 1005 is in both the first and second purchaser data-sets. That is, because this customer purchased once that will help model those who did not purchase. And because this customer purchased once they are in the 'predicting the second purchase' data-set. Tedious, but it will give us a way to predict everyone's total number of purchases for the next, say, two years. We will call lifetime value to be two years out.'

Mark nodded. 'Whew,' he sighed.

'Yes, it's a big job but can you see how valuable this will be?'

'In a couple of ways. First is the insights that by-segment/by-product marketing can understand what makes a customer valuable and what does not. That is, what levers drive value?'

'Absolutely. This makes it actionable.'

'Then we can score the database by segment by product with WHEN the next purchase is likely to happen and marcomm can use that to efficiently message at the appropriate time for the appropriate product.'

'Yes, I had not exactly thought of that,' Scott furrowed his brow. 'Good idea.'

'Using tobit also means we can apply the same approach to purchase amount as well as timing. And then we will all need to take a vacation.'

Scott laughed. 'Agreed!'

The following week Scott and Mark presented the results of the LTV model to senior management. They decided to show the consumer electronics model (Table 14.3). This product had fairly high margin and was important in the upcoming fourth-quarter promotions. And the merchandizers had bought a large inventory of giant screen TVs to allow assortment to better compete.

TABLE 14.3   LTV: model output (consumer electronics)

	COEFF	ODS RATIO	IMPACT	AVERAGE
5% DISCOUNT	−0.600	0.549	−45%	−5.189
Q2	+0.880	2.411	141%	+16.225
Q3	+1.330	3.781	278%	+31.982
Q4	−0.522	0.593	−41%	−4.677
SPEAKER BUNDLE	−0.350	0.705	−30%	−3.396
# DIR MAILS	−0.026	0.974	−3%	−0.295
# E-MAILS	+0.123	1.130	13%	+1.499
AVG WEEK TTE	11.5			

'This table shows the general impact of a 5 per cent price discount, bundling, marcomm and seasonality on our consumer electronics market,' Scott said.

'How do I use this? What does it mean?' asked a serious-minded marketer, who was obviously motivated by greed, which Scott appreciated.

Scott nodded. 'This model says that the average time until the event – in this case a consumer electronics purchase – is about 11.5 weeks. A 5 per cent discount tends to BRING IN the purchase by 5.189 weeks. Just seasonality alone also has an impact; for example, in Q2 it pushes out the purchase by 16.225 weeks.'

'So these effects are additive? That is, if we promote a bundle we bring in by 3.396 weeks and a 5 per cent discount brings in AN ADDITIONAL 5.189 weeks? Meaning bringing in by nearly 8.5 weeks?'

'Yes, on average,' Scott smiled.

'But,' the finance guy pointed out, 'What is the cost of a 5 per cent discount? How much margin are we losing?'

The marketer looked at him. 'We get over 40 per cent margin on each giant screen TV, not that that is the only product in the consumer electronics category, but there seems to be room to give away 5 per cent. I think the overall average margin is probably 30 per cent at least.'

'And,' Scott said, 'that brings a purchase in by over 5 weeks, so they have a chance to make another overall purchase. That is, if our customers make about 4.5 purchases in consumer electronics a year, by shortening the cycle we might be able to squeeze one more purchase out of them, maybe 5.5 average per year.'

'Or,' the finance guy again leaned forward, 'we have simply brought their Q1 purchases into Q4 and our Q1 forecast will now be off.'

Scott shrugged. 'That's obviously a strategic question. But there's more to this than a Q4 consumer electronics promotion. This is really about LTV. We have done a similar model on all of our customers for all of our major product categories. We have overall found similar results: a discount tends to bring in a purchase – shortening the cycle, increasing overall value, seasonality as a driver, bundling (using market basket techniques) seems to aid.'

'That's a lot of work.'

'Yes, but now we have the database scored by LTV. So we can target those that are lower valued by these actions, thereby increasing their overall value.'

TABLE 14.4   Tobit output

CUSTOMER	PURCH	AMOUNT	PRED
1000	0		0
1002	0		0
1003	0		270
1005	1	450	420
1007	1	275	220
1009	0		0
1011	0		150
1013	1	175	140
1015	1	575	650
1019	1	450	400
1021	1	225	220
1023	0		190
1025	0		0
1030	0		0
1032	1	175	180
1034	1	550	520

'And because we know, for example,' pointed out the finance guy, 'what the cost is of a discount, there is a business case to be made. It cost us this much to market to a low-valued customer but if they take the promotion their value increases in order to offset the cost.'

The marketer smiled. 'That means a positive ROI!'

The finance guy looked at him.

'Yes, marketers know what an ROI is,' he laughed. 'But this is just predicting when a customer will buy next, and even how many times in the future – which is great. But that is not all of lifetime value. How much do they purchase?'

Scott nodded. 'Exactly. This addresses the timing of a purchase. Typically, analytics will just assume the past continues into the future, that is, the volume of the purchase, amplitude, is the same as the historical past. This is a pretty heroic assumption.'

'And it's only descriptive,' Mark pointed out.

'Right,' Scott said. 'We want to get to predictive as soon as, and as often as, possible. Using a technique called tobit analysis, which essentially predicts the amount of a purchase – even of those that have not purchased – allows us to better estimate LTV. And, as with all regressions, gives independent variables – levers – for you to pull to increase a customer's value, or understand why a customer is lower valued.'

Mark changed the slide, showing Table 14.4. 'Here is how it looks on the database.' He showed which customers have not purchased and how tobit estimates the amount.

'But there is not a prediction for everyone,'

'Right,' said Scott. 'Some of them are still predicted to NOT purchase. And this is of strategic interest to you, this is how we calculate LTV.'

Everyone around the table looked at each other. No one looked at their phone.

'Well,' said the head marketer, 'let's put this in a field test. Good job.'

Conclusion

What survival analysis offers, in addition to marketing strategy levers, is a financial optimal scenario, particularly in terms of costs to market. That is, customer X responds to a discount. It's possible to calculate and test what is the (just) needed threshold of discounts to bring a purchase in by so many days with the estimated level of revenue. This ends up being a cost/benefit analysis that makes marketers think about strategy. This is the advantage of predictive analysis: giving marketers strategic options.

Another strategically lucrative use is in terms of lifetime value. While it's often calculated using only historical descriptive data, using survival modelling gives two advantages: puts it in the predictive (quantifying causality) phase and supplies marketing 'levers' to change customer LTV.

Checklist

You'll be the smartest person in the room if you:

☐ Point out the differences (advantages) of using predictive modelling (survival analysis) over descriptive analysis in estimating lifetime value (LTV).

☐ Remember one of the biggest advantages of predictive LTV is that independent variables (eg number of e-mails sent, change in price, bundling options) can provide marketers with a quantitative lever to use to increase an individual customer's LTV.

☐ Keep in mind that retail has multiple events, so there will need to be a different model for each event. That is, a model for time until first purchase, another model for time until second purchase, another model for time until third purchase, etc.

☐ Advocate doing tobit to predict volume (revenue) of those that have not purchased instead of ordinary regression.

MODELLING COUNTS 15 (TRANSACTIONS)

MARKETING QUESTION

What can I use to explain number of transactions, number of purchases, etc?

ANALYTIC SOLUTION

Poisson regression

A common analytic question is to understand movement in the number of transactions, or counts of purchases. This is a minor but important point, especially to the extent that zeros are in the dependent variable. For example, if you are trying to model number of transactions and if the sensitivity of the independent variables is key (as it should be) Poisson regression is a better choice than ordinary regression.

The Poisson process has the property that the distribution of the number of eg transactions in any interval depends only on the length of that interval. Conceptually, Poisson regression is a dependent-variable technique that uses a distribution other than the normal distribution on which OLS is based. It uses the Poisson distribution, which is a way to describe count data:

$$\frac{\lambda^k}{k!}e^{-\lambda}$$

This distribution measures the probability of a variable, say X, to be k where k is the count from 0 to n. It states that this probability is chosen using the parameter λ (lamda). k! is k factorial and e is the constant 2.71828. λ can be interpreted as the rate of the process. (I suppose if lamda is meaningless, it provides no relevance, doesn't speak to us and we can call it the silence of the lamda.) The point being, to the extent the timing of the events follow independently, is the extent that this distribution measures the data generating process. So Poisson regression posits the dependent (count) variable comes from the above Poisson distribution. It uses a maximum likelihood technique as does for example logistic regression. Mathematically the logarithm of its mean is modelled by the independent variables, βXi. The random variable (Y_{it}) – which is the number of transactions by consumer i in a particular time period t – then follows a Poisson distribution with parameter λ:

$$P(Y_{it}) = f(yit \mid \lambda, t) = \frac{e^{-\lambda t}(\lambda t)^{yit}}{yit!}$$

So, why do we care about this? Why just add yet another kind of regression? Because it more accurately models/fits the behaviour we're interested in understanding/quantifying.

Business case

One of Scott's analysts, Meenu, knocked on his door.

'Hi,' he said. 'What's up?'

'I have a model that seems to work,' Meenu said, 'but it gives a very large impact to e-mail, which the marketers say they know is of nearly irrelevant effectiveness.'

'OK, hold it,' Scott smiled, 'sit down. Now tell me what you're doing.'

Meenu sat on the chair and spun her laptop toward him. 'This is for our crochet and knitting department. They've asked me to do a model to help allocate the direct mail and e-mail and SMS budget.'

Scott nodded his head.

Meenu continued. 'They say they know that e-mail is not effective...'.

'Yes, probably the targeted age is of those NOT using e-mail.'

'Right. And the model I have is showing e-mail as pretty strong.' She pointed to an ordinary regression output. She showed him the model in Table 15.1 which had number of transactions as the dependent variable.

TABLE 15.1   Ordinary regression output

Variable	Parameter Estimate	Standard Error	t Value	Pr > |t|
net price	–2.52717	0.09698	–26.06	<.0001
# dir mails	0.11009	0.00353	31.21	<.0001
#sms	0.20968	0.03209	6.53	<.0001
#e-mails	0.13984	0.00559	25.04	<.0001
hh income	0.00872	0.00351	2.49	0.0130

'So this says for 1,000 e-mails sent we get 139 transactions. That does seem high,' Scott said. 'What is the purchase frequency distribution of crochet and knitting products?'

Meenu produced Figure 15.1.

'Yes,' Scott said. 'It's a counting distribution.'

Meenu furrowed her brow. 'Counting distribution?'

'You used OLS which seems to make sense, except that it uses the normal distribution which assumes the mean = the median = mode and is symmetrical, the bell-shaped curve. This is NOT a normal distribution, but a skewed distribution. What is the mean value here?'

'2.15' she said.

'Yes, now tell me: is 2.15 the most representative number?'

'Most representative? No. The most representative number is closer to 1.00.'

'Right. Use the Poisson distribution and you will see a change in fit for the better and a change in coefficients, hopefully also for the better.'

'How do I do that?'

FIGURE 15.1   Number of transactions

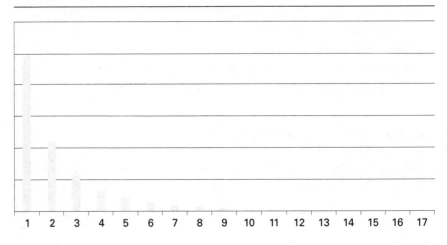

'Like this,' Scott said and took hold of her keyboard. After getting a few details he wrote this SAS code:

```
proc countreg data=xxx;
 model total_trans = net price n_dm n_em n_sms
 hhincome/dist=poisson ;
 run;
```

Scott showed her the results in Table 15.2.

TABLE 15.2   Poisson regression output

Parameter	Estimate	Standard Error	t Value	Pr > |t|
net price	−0.886146	0.044604	−19.87	<.0001
# dir mails	0.295020	0.015571	18.95	<.0001
# sms	0.166299	0.017708	9.39	<.0001
# e-mails	0.004203	0.000235	17.84	<.0001
hh income	0.010133	0.001955	5.18	<.0001

'Interpret the impact like logistic regression:

$$(e^B - 1) * \text{mean of } 1.1'$$

'Wow,' Meenu smiled. 'Now 1,000 e-mails drive only 4.6 transactions.'
'And direct mail has become more important, probably as it should be.'
Meenu sighed and smiled. 'This makes much more sense. Thanks.'

'Sure,' Scott said. 'Let me see the PowerPoint output when you're finished.'

She waved and picked up her laptop and walked out. Scott loved it when he could help, which was not often enough.

Conclusion

Poisson regression is appropriate where the dependent variable is count data. In retail this is typically number of transactions, number of responses or number of visits. When the count gets sufficiently large (whatever large means) a return to OLS is fine. Usually a graph can be done of the count data and to the extent it looks normal is the extent that OLS can be used. Or if the skewness metric is close to zero, Poisson can be abandoned.

Checklist

You'll be the smartest person in the room if you:

☐ Advocate using Poisson regression when modelling count data.

☐ Remember to diagnose how 'normal' the variable is by using both skewness and graphing methods.

QUANTIFYING COMPLEXITY OF CUSTOMER BEHAVIOUR 16

MARKETING QUESTION

How does price (or other stimuli) affect different brands (or product)? Are there stages of impact?

ANALYTIC SOLUTION

Simultaneous equations

Introduction

So far we've dealt with one equation, a rather simple point of view. Of course, consumer behaviour is anything but simple. Marketing science is designed to understand and predict and ultimately incentivize and change consumer behaviour. This requires techniques that are as complicated as that behaviour is sophisticated. This is where simultaneous equations come in, as a more realistic model of behaviour.

What are simultaneous equations?

Simply put, simultaneous equations are systems of equations. You had this in algebra. It's important. This begins to build a simulation of an entire process. It's done in macroeconomics (remember the Keynesian equations?). And it can be done in marketing.

Predetermined and exogenous variables

There are two kinds of variables: predetermined (lagged endogenous and exogenous) and endogenous variables. Generally, exogenous are variables determined OUTSIDE the system of equations and endogenous are determined INSIDE the system of equations. (Think of endogenous variables as being explained by the model.) This comes in handy to know when using the rule in the identity problem below. (The identity problem is a GIANT pain in the neck but the model cannot be estimated without going through these hoops.)

This is important because a predetermined variable is one that is contemporaneously uncorrelated with the error term in its equation. Note how this ties up with causality. If Y is caused by X, then Y cannot be an independent variable in contemporaneously predicting/explaining Y.

Say we have a system common in economics:

$$Q(demand) = D(I) + D(price) + Income + D(error)$$
$$Q(supply) = S(I) + S(price) + S(error)$$

Note that the variables Q and price are endogenous (computed within the system) and income is exogenous. That is, income is given. (D(I) is the intercept in the demand equation and S(I) is the intercept in the supply equation. D(error) is the error term in the demand equation and S(error) is the error term in the supply equation.) These equations are called structural forms of the model. Algebraically, these structural forms can be solved for endogenous variables giving a reduced form of the equations. That is:

$$Q = \left(\frac{D(price) * S(I) - D(I) * S(price)}{D(price) - S(price)} \right) - \left(\frac{Income * S(price)}{D(price) - S(price)} \right) Income$$
$$+ \left(\frac{-S(price) * D(error) + D(price) * S(error)}{D(price) - S(price)} \right)$$

$$p = \left(\frac{-D(I) + S(I)}{D(price) - S(price)} \right) - \left(\frac{Income}{D(price) - S(price)} \right) Income + \left(\frac{-D(error) + S(error)}{D(price) - S(price)} \right)$$

The reduced form of the equations shows how the endogenous variables (those determined within the system) DEPEND on the predetermined variables and error terms. That is, the values of Q and P are explicitly determined by income and errors. This means that income is given to us.

Note that the endogenous variable price appears as an independent variable in each equation. In fact, it is NOT independent, it depends on income and error terms and this is the issue. It is specifically correlated with its own (contemporaneous) error term. Correlation of an independent variable and its error terms leads to inconsistent results.

Why go to the trouble to use simultaneous equations?

First, because it's fun. Also note that if a system should be modelled with simultaneous equations and IS NOT, the parameter estimates are INCONSISTENT! Lastly, insights are more realistic. The simulation suggests the appropriate complexity.

Second, staging (dependent variables in one equation feeding as independent variables in another equation) is how consumer behaviour operates. For example, staging is seen when price impacts satisfaction and satisfaction impacts units. Note that in this example satisfaction can be a dependent variable as well as an independent variable, an issue which we'll get to soon enough.

Conceptual basics

Generally, any economic model has to have the number of variables with values to be explained to be equal to the number of independent relationships in the model. This is the identification problem.

Many textbooks (Kmenta, Kennedy, Greene, etc) can give the mathematic derivation for the solution of simultaneous equations. The general problem is that there have to be enough known variables to 'fix' each unknown quantity estimated. That is, there needs to be a rule. The good news is that there is. Here is the rule for solving the identification problem:

The number of predetermined variables excluded in the equation MUST be >= the number of endogenous variables included in the equation, less one.

Let's use this rule on the supply–demand equation above:

$$Q(demand) = D(l) + D(price) + Income + D(error)$$
$$Q(supply) = S(l) + S(price) + S(error)$$

Demand: the number of predetermined variables excluded = zero. Income is the only predetermined variable and it IS NOT excluded from the demand equation. The number of endogenous variables included less one = 2 − 1 = 1. The two endogenous variables are quantity and price. So the number of predetermined variables excluded in the equation = 0 and this is < the number of endogenous variables included in the equation. Therefore, the demand equation is under-identified.

Supply: the number of predetermined variables excluded = one. Income is the only predetermined variable and it is excluded from the supply equation. The number of endogenous variables included less one = 2 − 1 = 1. The two endogenous variables are quantity and price. So the number of predetermined variables excluded in the equation = 0 and this is < the number of endogenous variables included in the equation. Therefore, the supply equation is exactly identified.

Simultaneous equation techniques

To get at a quick overview of techniques, we need to define instrumental variables. We have already defined endogenous and exogenous variables. We will now look at a popular single-equation technique that addresses simultaneity bias. Then we will overview a systems/multi-equation approach.

In two-stage least squares (2SLS) ordinary regression is done on reduced form equations (those equations where each endogenous variable is regressed on all exogenous variables). This is Stage 1. The second stage uses these fitted endogenous variables as estimators for the final stage. That is, put these fitted/estimated regressions back into the structural equations and run regression on these.

For example, assume we have four variables (this is just an algebraic, not a business, exercise): W, X, Y and Z. Assume the structural equations are:

$$W = X + Y + lagW$$
$$X = Y + W + Z$$

This gives us the following reduced form equations:

$$W^* = Y + lagW + Z$$
$$X^* = Y + lagW + Z$$

Estimating the fitted endogenous variables above is Stage 1. Now run OLS as Stage 2 using the fitted values placed back into the structural equations:

$$W = X^* + Y + lagW$$
$$X = Y + W^* + Z$$

Where X^* and W^* are the estimated values. Thus, 2SLS is a single-equation method of combatting the 'independent variables fixed in repeated samples' assumption.

To clarify, the usual equation in a simultaneous equation system has (at least) one endogenous variable used as an independent variable, that is, as a regressor. This is a violation of the ordinary regression assumption of 'non-stochastic X': that is, this endogenous variable cannot be considered as fixed in repeated samples. This assumption asserts it is possible to generate the sample with the same independent variable values. In a simultaneous equation system, all endogenous variables are stochastic. This means a change in an error term changes all of the endogenous variables since they are solved simultaneously.

Three-stage least squares (3SLS) is an extension of 2SLS. Summarizing the process:

- Stage 1: calculate the 2SLS estimates of the (identified) equations.
- Stage 2: use the 2SLS estimates to estimate the structural equation's error terms and then use these to estimate the

contemporaneous variance–covariance (VCV) matrix of the structural equation's error terms.

- Stage 3: model (using these transformed equations) this large equation representing all the (identified) equations of the system.

The standard errors of the 3SLS systems are smaller than the same equations using 2SLS. But be aware the only desirable property of these parameter estimates is consistency.

Unfortunately, I am required by 'law' to mention VAR. VAR is vector autoregression. (A professor I had called it 'very awful regressions'!) In simple terms VAR hypothesizes that all the variables in the system are endogenous and they are linear functions of their own lagged values and all the lagged values of all other variables. These are now a vector (including residuals). The vector of all dependent variables can be regressed on all independent variables as in any OLS.

VAR has its advocates, especially among econometric time series forecasters. When the only requirement is to forecast some dependent variable, maybe VAR is acceptable.

My issue with it is that by mathematical definition all the dependent variables have the same independent variables and that seems to be a causality issue. Also it is impossible to get a coefficient (a measure of impact) on any one independent variable on its associated dependent variable. (VAR does not even have t-ratios!) From a structural analysis point of view (which is where most marketing happens) VAR does not/cannot provide any insights.

Business case

Scott received an urgent meeting request for the next morning from their customer insights team. This was a predominantly marketing research organization. This team typically designed primary research and brand tracking surveys in terms of path to purchase, satisfaction, loyalty, advertising and marcomm awareness, competitive density, etc.

Scott walked into the director's office.

'Oh, you've arrived,' said a middle-aged woman very smartly dressed. 'Come on in and have a seat. I'm Jean.'

Scott shook her hand and sat down.

She smiled. 'I wanted to brainstorm with you – per Becky's suggestion – on a couple of projects we have coming up.'

'Great,' Scott said taking out his notebook and pen. 'Go ahead.'

'Well the first one comes from head of merchandizing.'

That immediately surprised Scott. Marketing (as typical in retail) reports up through merchandizing. That is, merchandizers rule the retail world and some of them virtually looked down at marketing organizations.

'I see,' he said.

'The chief merchandizing officer wants to ascertain the right level of staffing in the stores. That is, if we can prove even the size of the staff has an impact on, say, basket size that can help us in hiring.'

Scott paused. 'So this is not about customer analytics?'

'The sample frame will be stores, that's true,' Jean said.

'So we're not trying to understand which kind of staff members to hire, that is, sales associates or store managers, but just the number of employees?'

'At this time, yes, just a proof-of-concept, that increasing staff members positively increases sales. Then if we find that to be true and test it next quarter we might dive in deeper with different titles/skills of employees.'

'Wow, sounds fun. So this is a store model. Do we have the data we need?'

'Well, what data do we need? We obviously have sales by store and a count of staff in each store.'

'We will need that. We have to think what causes sales and by that I mean number of units. We'll ignore product type for now and just model units.'

'Units? You mean quantity of products sold?'

'Yes, we posit all the things that might impact units: staff number is the dimension of interest but we also have to include things like net price and marcomm sent and seasonality.'

'But why units? Not revenue?'

'As an econ guy my bias is to believe that net price has a strong impact on purchasing.'

'Sure.'

'Because revenue is units multiplied by net price, net price cannot be on both sides of the equation.'

'I suppose that's true,' she sighed. 'We also know from our own brand tracking that satisfaction affects sales, that is, units.'

'Yes, I'm sure it does. This is getting complicated.'

She looked thoughtful. 'This one question is creeping into a very big project.'

'But real important,' Scott said, leaning forward and getting excited by the possibilities. 'What affects store performance? Is it net price, that is price after discounts, or is it size of staff, or is it satisfaction, or is it seasonality...'.

'And the answer is that for some stores it IS net price based on competitive density and social economics/demographics but for another store it is satisfaction which is caused by both net price and staffing.'

'Clearly this is out of marketing analytics. It's more about finance/real estate, or operations.'

She smiled. 'Yes, and merchandizing?'

Scott shrugged. 'Yes, this is big. We may end up simulating our entire business.' Now a realization hit Scott. 'We will have to have multiple equations. Perhaps an equation for units and a different equation for maybe satisfaction because, as you said, price and staffing impact satisfaction and that, in another stage, impacts units. Price also has a direct link to units.'

She shook her head. 'I'm not sure what you mean.'

'Well, we'll have to design this based on causality but right now I'd say it might look like this.' Scott wrote on the board the following equations:

$$\text{Units} = f(\text{satisfaction, net price, staffing, marcomm})$$
$$\text{Satisfaction} = f(\text{net pricing, staffing})$$

They both stared at the board and then shrugged. 'This involves multiple equations. Are you acquainted with SEM? Structural equation modelling?' she asked.

'Barely. I think that is about multiple equations but an important difference is that SEM is powerful in hypothesizing latent variables, hidden variables. It does not seem like we need to address that here; none of our variables, as discussed, are hidden, but blatant. I have more of an econometric view anyway and our approach will be first to test simultaneous equations.'

'OK,' she said. 'You guys get to work and we'll start this project.'

Scott was about to stand up when he remembered what she said. 'You mentioned two projects?'

She nodded. 'Yes, the second one is on loyalty modelling, probably even more complicated than this. We'll talk later.'

'My head hurts,' he smiled. 'That might be about SEM.'

'I'll send you some pain killers. Let's get back together when you have some output.'

Scott sighed and walked back to his office. He pulled out his notes and files and textbook on simultaneous equations. He also pulled out of the bottom drawer of his desk a one-foot square cork board. He taped it next to his white board. He would be pounding his head on that cork board over the next few weeks.

Scott collected the data he needed. It included survey data from the stores around customer satisfaction, customer services and employee engagement. He got a count of staffing at each store. This included function and titles, although he would not use that yet. He collected average net price by store and average units (to multiply by price to get revenue) and marcomm sent. Marcomm included number of direct mails to each of the store's customers, number of e-mails and number of SMS. He got trade area data around each store in terms of social economic variables, demographics and competitive density.

He drew Figure 16.1 as the updated model's structural equations. There were still two equations: one had a dependent variable of units and the other had the dependent variable of satisfaction. One key thing is that net price is in both models, that is, net price is an endogenous variable used as an independent variable. Simultaneous equations will solve the impact of net price in terms of BOTH equations. Another key thing is that satisfaction is both a dependent as well as an independent variable. That is, satisfaction feeds into units, which is again the definition of requiring simultaneous equations.

After a couple of weeks of difficulty, he had a framework (Figure 16.1) for each equation that seemed to make sense. He collected data. Marcomm would be direct mail, e-mail, SMS and newspaper inserts. Staffing would be a count and title. Employee engagement and customer service and satisfaction came from a quarterly survey. Competitive density and social economics/demographics was from a third party. He would have to apply these equations to each store. He would do a model by both national and regional level.

The identification problem was not too difficult to solve. He had enough variables to add/subtract as needed. The biggest difficulty was, of course,

FIGURE 16.1 Conceptual model framework

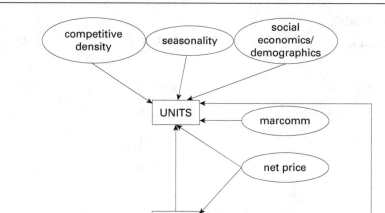

in collinearity. Most of the variables came with a strong hypothesis of sign (eg as satisfaction increased units should also increase). But after considerable use of VIF and the condition index he found what seemed to fit well and most of the variables expected to be significant were with the hypothesized signs.

He did the west region first, being the largest and most important region. Table 16.1 shows the output of the model. First, note the satisfaction model. All the variables positively influence the level of customer satisfaction, including staffing. That is, if the number of staff increases, the satisfaction also tends to increase. But see the p-value on satisfaction is 21 per cent, or significant at the 79 per cent level? This might mean it is not really important. (Yes we can (and should) dive deeper into the granularity of staffing, especially the KINDS of staff hired: is a manager more impactful than a clerk?) It's obvious there is an ROI or business case here: what is the cost of increasing staff given the benefit of increasing satisfaction?

Now look at the unit model. Satisfaction is positive as hypothesized, net price is negative (as hypothesized) and significant. E-mail is NEGATIVE. (This is found fairly often, especially in retail circles. Retailers e-mail WAY

TABLE 16.1   Simultaneous equations: model output (west region)

UNIT MODEL

VARIABLE	ESTIMATE	P VAL
Units		
Satisfaction	+0.0514	0.0989
Net price	−6.8809	0.0022
Direct mail	+0.0015	0.0306
E-mail	−0.0004	0.09081
SMS	+0.0024	0.11566
NPI	+0.0156	0.15157
Staffing	+0.0207	0.0894
# Competitors	−1.0054	0.00056
HH income	+0.0007	0.2215
% unemployment	−2.0335	0.30215
Q2	1,002	0.0253
Q3	1,588	0.0015
Q4	2,908	0.068

SATISFACTION MODEL

VARIABLE	ESTIMATE	P VAL
Satisfaction		
Customer Service	+2.0665	0.00265
Employee engagement	+0.0066	0.2154
Staffing	+0.0909	0.21506
Net price	+1.0220	0.0332

too much, they somehow think it is cost-less. But e-mail fatigue is real and this model can quantify how a growing number of e-mails tends to DECREASE the number of units sold.) Most importantly, note that staffing is positive and significant at about the 91 per cent level. This indicates that as staffing increases, units will also increase. Again there is a business case here to be quantified. What is the cost of the average staff? As 100 staff are added to the western region that will add 2.07 units (per store per year). So, is it worth it?

Scott calculated elasticity by the region $(-6.88) * 75 / 460) = -1.1219$, so this region is generally elastic and sensitive to price. This means that to increase total revenue stores should generally DECREASE price. Now we can see what the stores actually did in terms of price changes and other operations.

Part of the power of this model is that Scott and his team can provide the general manager with a store 'scorecard', where the model shows which variables are important and in what direction to move them. Then a store's performance can be matched against operations and an improvement plan can be generated.

Look at the scorecard in Table 16.2 and note the top and bottom store performances. Note the column YOY REV CHANGE shows what percentage change each store had this year compared to last year. This is the metric to focus on, because so much of retail is about same store sales, or year over year changes. With this the general manager can make individual store changes and ascertain if an individual store is carrying its own weight.

Let's follow a couple of store scorecards. The unit model above shows that net price is a very significant variable in terms of moving units – which directly impact total revenue. A price elasticity calculation showed this region to be generally sensitive to price (at 1.1219). Thus the right move would tend to decrease price. Note that for all the top stores a YOY change in price was downward. Marcomm spend (an index of each store to the overall average) was greater than average for two of the top three stores. Lastly the question of interest was about staff increases. Again two out of the top three stores had an increase in staffing. These (and other metrics) seem to tell the story that successful stores face both dimensions they can control and some they can't. But if they move the dimension they can control in the way suggested by the model they have a better chance for success.

TABLE 16.2 Scorecard

	YOY REV CHANGE	YOY SAT CHANGE	YOY PRICE CHANGE	MARCOMM INDEX	YOY # STAFF CHANGE	# COMP INDEX	HH INCOME INDEX	% UNEMPLOY
WEST REGION 12	+6.6%	+0.1%	-2.3%	112%	+2.3%	77%	98%	87%
WEST REGION 13	+2.6%	+0.2%	-4.5%	131%	+5.4%	65%	87%	99%
WEST REGION 9	+0.3%	+3.5%	-1.1%	99%	-2.0%	112%	115%	75%
WEST REGION 10	-0.8%	-11.2%	-3.2%	144%	-9.6%	34%	145%	123%
WEST REGION 11	-2.7%	-65.6%	+1.0%	54%	-7.8%	144%	65%	155%
WEST REGION 17	-8.8%	-3.6%	+2.0%	85%	+1.1%	165%	99%	144%
WEST REGION 20	-11.2%	+2.2%	-2.7%	123%	-7.4%	88%	87%	87%

Look now at the stores that were not so successful, as measured by YOY revenue change. In terms of pricing half of them RAISED prices – clearly a wrong move! Half of them (#11 and #17) spend less on marcomm and three out of the bottom four had fewer staff. Now it's also true that three out of four faced higher than average unemployment and lower household income. Half of them had more than average number of competitors. This would indicate that stores in difficult economic areas should REALLY focus on those dimensions they can control: pricing, marcomm spend, staffing, and so on.

Lastly, let's think about satisfaction and its impact on units which impact total revenue. Pricing and staffing are metrics in the unit model as well. Remember, this is the result of a survey and pricing here is NOT the direction of price but how survey respondents feel about price and its relationship to their satisfaction. All three of the top stores increased their satisfaction rating (partly because of their lowering prices and increasing staffing) and three of the bottom four performers (#10, #11 and #17) decreased their satisfaction ratings. The satisfaction model shows that employee engagement and customer service are also key factors in terms of satisfaction. From a business case point of view, in order to increase satisfaction these two dimensions also have to increase. There needs to be a deep dive into the details around employee engagement and customer services but it is clear that in order to increase these factors there is a cost: employee training, upgraded billing systems, service resolution, staff training, amongst others. Thus one of the key uses of this kind of modelling is from a portfolio theory perspective. Each regional general manager has a budget and they can allocate those dollars in the most impactful way: whether increasing marcomm, hiring more staff, training/educating staff, or upgrading computer billing systems.

Scott couldn't wait to show the director this (and the rest) of the output. She was very excited and would get the chief merchandizing officer in a meeting the following week. She also said she would use Scott and his team again, next month, on a loyalty problem, probably also involving multiple equations.

She did ask Scott about his approach using survey data. One insidious problem is missing values. Scott had a few ideas.

A brief note on missing value imputation

A common issue in survey data (as well as database data, but less so) is what to do about missing values. It is a typical practice (but as is the case with most typical practices, not a good idea) to just replace the missing value with the mean value. That is, assume we have survey data around demographics, including age. Say that in this case age is important to what we're studying. If a very small percentage of age data is missing, maybe replacing the missing values with the overall mean is not so bad. But it's still unwise.

A better solution is to do segmentation (even K-means is a decent choice) and based on, say, income and size of household, replace the missing age values with the mean of each segment. This indicates that age is correlated with income and size of household and that's probably not a bad assumption.

The best idea would be to model, using ordinary regression, the predicted age based on the above demographics by each segment. This would add variation, rather than only the (segment) mean value.

This is all based on a subjective idea that depends on the percentage of whatever value is missing. For example, if < 5 per cent is missing, replacing with the overall mean value might be acceptable. If between 5 and 25 per cent is missing, replacing with the mean value by segment is better. If between 25 and 50 per cent is missing, modelling the missing value with regression by segment is the best. If > 50 per cent is missing no imputation should be attempted.

The above are fast and simple ways to singly impute a missing value and these are often good enough, especially if there are very few missing values. But the most common/accepted idea of imputing missing values is with some kind of multiply-imputed procedure. It is this data-generating process that has the most sophistication. Multiply-imputed techniques create a random sample of missing values and then analyse the results giving confidence intervals to assess risk. This is especially true when a large number of important variables are missing. The most common practice (in SAS) is through:

```
PROC MI DATA = XX.XX MCMC IMPUTE = (either monotone
or full imputation)
VAR = (X1,X1...Xn variables to impute); RUN;
```

MCMC uses a Markov Chain Monte Carlo technique, assuming an arbitrary missing pattern and a multivariate normal distribution. This usually suffices.

Conclusion

Simultaneous equations is an advanced econometric technique that gives complexity to a system. The advantages are that one equation can be modelled to 'feed' into another equation. Another advantage is that one (or more) independent variables can be a dependent variable in another equation. This additional reality, while increasing sophistication, allows a better theory of causality.

Checklist

You'll be the smartest person in the room if you:

- [ ] Learn to enjoy the added complexity that simultaneous equations bring to analytics – the technique better matches consumer behaviour.

- [ ] Remember that simultaneous equations use two kinds of variables: predetermined (endogenous and lagged exogenous) and exogenous variables.

- [ ] Point out that estimators have desirable properties such as unbiasedness, efficiency, consistency.

- [ ] Prove that simultaneous equations can be used for optimal pricing and understanding cannibalization between products, brands, etc.

- [ ] Are willing to hypothesize and model a staged structure, eg one variable may feed into another variable.

DESIGNING EFFECTIVE LOYALTY PROGRAMMES

17

MARKETING QUESTION

What are the issues with loyalty, programme design and analytics? How do I take advantage of and model the 'earn–burn' rate?

ANALYTIC SOLUTION

Loyalty design and survival modelling for earn–burn

Introduction to loyalty

So, what is loyalty? We all know what it is, so shouldn't it be easy to define? In the context of analytics, loyalty is when a consumer becomes a customer and likes the brand enough to come back again. This customer likes the brand enough to continue coming back and even spread the word to their family and friends, even recommend it to their peers and network, even be an ambassador for the brand. Note that at its base loyalty is about the customer, it is NOT about the firm or brand. That is, loyalty analytics is (as it always should be) focussed on the customer – what does the customer need, what does the customer like, what is the customer sensitive to, what will it take for the customer to become emotionally involved with the brand, what touch points are most important to a customer? Often this means defining loyalty in terms of customer segments, especially how loyal a segment is, which needs or benefits does the brand satisfy for one segment over another, what is the range of loyalty – is it merely transactionally loyal or is a segment emotionally involved as an ambassador for the brand?

So the first issue is that loyalty should be designed as a win–win and viewed primarily from the customer's point of view, not the firm's. Note that most loyalty analytics, and even most loyalty books (even the pillar of loyalty books, Reichheld's *The Loyalty Effect*) is mostly about the firm. That position tries to explain why loyalty helps a firm, how a firm should be interested in loyalty, what metrics should the firm track to gauge its customer's loyalty, how understanding loyalty and increasing loyalty is a benefit to the firm. This is short-sighted. This approach will produce only a pareto effect achieved quickly and never increased.

While loyalty no doubt has an important value to the firm, the right framework is obsessing on the customer: their experience, their wants or needs, what is valuable to THEM. This has everything to do with programme design. Why would a firm put a loyalty programme in place? If a firm is trying to collect members in order to send them e-mails about promotions and discounts, that is NOT a loyalty programme, it is an e-mail club. That may have some value, especially if the firm's products require a discount in order to buy, but that should not be called a loyalty programme. One thing to learn when understanding loyalty from a customer's perspective is that not all customers want the same thing, not all customers care about a discount. (This is what elasticity modelling is all about.) Some of them want something else! Remember, there are four Ps in tactical marketing and PRICE is only one of them.

Is there a range or spectrum of loyalty?

There is a range of loyalty from none to transactional to emotional. The point of loyalty analytics is to understand where on this spectrum a customer or segment is and learn how to incentivize and change their behaviour to move up the scale. If done right, this is not only for the customer's or segment's benefit, it is of benefit to the firm. Some customers or segments will not move, or it costs too much to get them to move on the spectrum, and that is a valuable insight!

Note that this is a problem in points-based loyalty programmes. They tend to reward the same behaviour. It's possible that that is all a customer and a firm want: identifying those high-end users and giving them a discount for continuing to purchase. It does NOT incentivize or reward incremental behaviour. Those who are low-end purchasers are not likely to become high-end purchasers just because of points.

What are the 3Rs of loyalty?

Bryan Pearson's *The Loyalty Leap* defined the 3Rs of loyalty as reward, recognition and relevance. But reward WHAT? The programme should be designed to reward incremental or new behaviour. Just rewarding (giving away margin) those that are already purchasing at a high level is a bad design. There will be no increased number of transactions but margin will be given away so the firm will show a net decrease in revenue. Remember, loyalty focusses on the customer in order to design a win–win programme. This is not altruism!

A good loyalty programme design will recognize incremental behaviour and reward it. In order to induce incremental behaviour the programme has to be relevant. This again references the above: not all customers demand a deep discount in order to induce loyalty. Some want other treatment.

A common example is from casual dining. A lot of so-called loyalty programmes are just e-mail clubs. The customer gives the waiter their e-mail and the waiter enters that into the system and then the customer begins getting a lot of e-mails (a LOT of e-mails!) offering discounts, price decreases, or promotions. (Note that in a few months e-mail fatigue, and even irritation, set in.) The restaurant gets more e-mails on their system and a way to send out discounts but it is of little value to the customers, except to get offers. The only customers this affects are those that are sensitive to price. It ignores exploiting or understanding any other lever or need or benefit.

A better approach is to design a system uniquely aimed at different customers' interests and needs. It is true some customers do want and need a discount and those customers are found via elasticity modelling. By the way, it is typical that those customers needing a discount in order to incrementally purchase are NOT usually the ones that are emotionally loyal to the brand, but only transactionally loyal.

There are some customers who are really not motivated by price to become loyal. Some customers will prefer better treatment. When they come into the restaurant they present their loyalty card and are allowed to 'jump to the front of the line', or they get a special table, or some kind of preferred treatment. Maybe they help design the menu, or have input into special dining experiences. This is what can help create emotional loyalty in an industry that has very little loyalty. Those customers that are potentially emotionally loyal can only be found through analytics and the programme design has to account for them.

Why design a programme with earn–burn measures?

This brings us to the 'earn–burn' metric. Earn is what rewards the customer has earned and burn is what rewards have been used. Earn is an accumulation of rewards, points, dollar values, tier status, etc. Burn typically focusses (especially in retail) on products or prestige. In casual dining, members earn rewards by purchasing products and they use their rewards to collect benefits (burn).

Part of a good design is to give the customer benefits they appreciate while still acknowledging the firm needs a benefit as well. For instance, it is well known in casual dining that the margin on alcohol is very high (75 per cent), whereas the margin on appetizers is much lower (20 per cent). But both products cost a similar amount. In this example the customer sees the cost of a drink is the same as an appetizer, but to the firm the margin is very different. Thus the firm should have the promos designed for the customer to EARN (purchase) alcohol in order to BURN (use rewards) on appetizers. The firm gets 75 per cent on earn and loses 20 per cent on burn. But the customer paid 5 for a drink and got 5 for an appetizer. Win–win.

The first step is finding the margin on categories of products. Table 17.1 shows some average retail margins. Now the programme design should separate the high margin (products members can EARN rewards on) from the low margin (products members are encouraged to BURN rewards on). The highest margin products are things like beauty aids, cards/books/ magazines, baby personal care, school office supplies. The lowest margin products are missy apparel, jewellery/watches, furniture, boy's apparel, girl's apparel, junior apparel, lawn/garden, men's apparel, patio furniture.

The idea is that for every 100 spent on, say, beauty aids and baby personal care, the member earns rewards and the firm gets a high margin. These rewards can be spent and burned on boy's apparel and patio furniture. The member is rewarded and the firm gives away low margin for the same spend. The appropriate product combination can be adjusted for strategy and inventory etc, but the idea is that the member is recognized and rewarded for incremental behaviour that is a win for the firm as well. Obviously different thresholds can be established to affect different behaviour and different goals for the firm. Focussing on the member's behaviour to understand and incentivize a change drives a benefit for the member as well as for the firm.

Now comes the analytic part: modelling when a member will earn and at what rate or amount as well as when a member will burn and at what rate or amount. The techniques used are typically survival modelling (remember it is about WHEN an event will happen) and ordinary regression can be used for the amount. It is also common to use logistic regression for the amount by turning the question into the probability of a threshold amount, rather than the continuous value of the amount.

Most analysts approach earn–burn modelling much as they approach time until purchases (see Chapter 14 on survival modelling). That is, the time until event is the dependent variable and the event (rather than a purchase) is either earn or burn. Often there is (much like purchase events) multiple earn and multiple burn events. Table 17.2 shows time until earning events – purchases made by a member. Again, in this regard, survival modelling is applied as LTV as time-until-first or time-until-second etc purchase. Note that a blank means the event has not happened – these events are censored.

TABLE 17.1 Category margin

	margin
Baby personal care	35%
Beauty aids	45%
Boy's apparel	15%
Cards, books, mags	40%
Consumer electronics	30%
Furniture	10%
Girl's apparel	15%
Home décor	25%
Home improvement	25%
Intimate apparel	20%
Jewellery, watches	10%
Junior apparel	15%
Kitchen, tabletop	20%
Lawn, garden	15%
Linens, domestics	20%
Men's apparel	15%
Missy apparel	10%
Newborn, infant	20%
Patio furniture	15%
School, office sup	35%
Small electronics	30%
Toys	30%
Women's accessories	25%

TABLE 17.2 Predicting time until each earn

CUSTOMER	TT 1 EARN	TT 2 EARN	TT 3 EARN	TT 4 EARN
1000	46	54	12	
1002	59	62	77	45
1004	12	41		
1006	88			
1009	125			
1012	45	65	78	
1015	65	44		
1018	3	15	24	34
1021	144	12		
1023	205	111	15	
1025	155			
1026	58	12		
1027	65			
1028	78	54	15	24
1029	88			
1030	115			
1034	305	14	48	
1038	45			

The real power comes when the event is a burn event – a using of rewards. Table 17.3 shows the time-until-burn event. The data-set has to be set up with flags and counts as shown. This is because a different model is applied to predict the first burn of those that currently have zero burn, the second burn of those that currently have only one burn, and so on.

TABLE 17.3   Database scored with time until each burn

CUSTOMER	TT 1 BURN	TT 2 BURN	TT 3 BURN
1000	34	5	
1002	15	24	35
1004			
1006			
1009	24		
1012			
1015			
1018	37	78	
1021			
1023	12		
1025			
1026	24	68	15
1027			
1028	44	12	
1029	15	89	
1030			
1034	48		
1038	114		

In the operating world the interest in the burn rate is behavioural pattern. This will differ by segment. Some members like to keep earning until they have a huge reward and then drastically burn it all away, others like to gain a little reward and then use a little reward. The win–win comes in the analytics exploiting this behaviour and offering incentives that dictate the pattern most favourable to the firm (note that stockpiling rewards is a liability to the firm) and most valuable to the members. Likewise, the ability to predict those members that will NEVER use their rewards is an important tool as well.

Business case

The loyalty group had been lobbying for some analytics around their customer members. After brainstorming it was decided that an understanding of earn–burn was a good step in developing a long-term strategy. This allowed personalizing for each member based on their behaviour and sensitivities and still maximized value to the firm. Scott designed a behavioural segmentation and an earn–burn model was applied to each segment. The segmentation was based on transactions and responses to marcomm, particularly around earning and burning rewards.

Scott showed the loyalty team Table 17.4, which shows two of the segments, X and Y. He pointed out how different their behaviour was in terms of time until the first burn. That is, since they became a member, how long and under what conditions was their first usage of their rewards. (This does not necessarily mean that they used ALL of their rewards, just how long until their reward balance decreased.)

'What do we do with this?' the director of loyalty asked.

Scott looked at her. 'What?'

'I see all these numbers in these tables but am not sure what to make of it.'

Scott rubbed his chin. 'I'm just showing two segments, now called X and Y, and the differences in their behaviour. Segment X's time-until-first burn is 4.55 months which is very different to Segment Y's time-until-first burn of 1.67 months.'

'Oh, so it's a prediction?'

'This is descriptive statistics, what actually happened in the past. But the model can be predictive. More importantly, it gives you levers to CHANGE the prediction.' He saw that she did not really get it. 'The important thing – besides a prediction – is that this is a kind of regression and as such has independent variables.'

'Right.' She furrowed her brow.

'These independent variables help explain the movement in the dependent variable, in this case time-until-first burn.'

'Sure, that makes sense.'

'It also tells what you can do with it. Note that in Segment X every direct mail sent brings in next time until burn by 0.515 months and every direct mail sent to Segment Y brings in time-until-first burn by 0.390 months. This means that you can move the time-until-first burn in

TABLE 17.4 Modelling time until first burn, by segment

TT FIRST BURN – SEGMENT X VARIABLE	COEFF	MONTHLY IMPACT
Earn Reward Amount	0.023	0.104
# of Visits	0.075	0.354
Time Between Visits	0.070	0.330
# of Categories Purch	−0.250	−1.006
% Earn / Burn Spend	−1.750	−3.759
# E-mails Sent	−0.399	−1.497
# Direct Mails Sent	−0.120	−0.515
# SMS Sent	−0.220	−0.899
Distance From Store	0.550	3.336
# of Competitors	0.670	4.342
AVERAGE MONTHLY TTE = 4.55		

TT FIRST BURN – SEGMENT Y VARIABLE	COEFF	MONTHLY IMPACT
Earn Reward Amount	−0.330	−0.469
# of Visits	−0.370	−0.516
Time Between Visits	0.190	0.349
# of Categories Purch	−1.767	−1.385
% Earn / Burn Spend	−3.750	−1.631
# E-mails Sent	−1.750	−1.380
# Direct Mails Sent	−0.266	−0.390
# SMS Sent	−0.570	−0.726
Distance From Store	0.403	0.830
# of Competitors	0.055	0.094
AVERAGE MONTHLY TTE = 1.67		

Segment X, from 4.55 to 4.035 (4.55 − 0.515) by sending more direct mails. Now there are a lot of things that go into it but this is how you use the model.'

'Oh, wow!' Her face twisted into a bright smile.

Scott nodded. She got it.

'So we can essentially manipulate burn rates by segment?'

'Well, in a sense,' Scott said. 'This is a model and a prediction but the relative scale is right and the direction is right. We did this for first burn and second burn on up to tenth burn.'

The director was engaged now. She e-mailed more of her team to come into the conference room. The rest of the day they strategized how to use this new information. Scott even showed tobit analysis, modelling the amount of earn–burn. It was a good day.

Conclusion

Customer loyalty is a crucial dimension for a firm's success. All too often the analytics around loyalty are carried out from the firm's point of view. This has a place but it should be in the background. The point of analytics is to understand and incentivize customer behaviour to create a win–win programme for both the firm and the customer. From the concept of Pearson's 3Rs comes a programme design that emphasizes the relevance of the rewards and recognizes incremental behaviour. That is, no programme should give away a firm's value to customers who just do what they have done before, and who just do what they would be doing in the future. The point of a loyalty programme is to drive incremental behaviour. This behaviour has to be monitored before and after the programme implementation so that customers' responses are changing their behaviour.

A large part of initial programme design is around the earn–burn metrics. Margin on each product category must be collected and customers are rewarded with low-margin products for purchasing high-margin products. Customers do not know what the margins are but the full price on both earn and burn categories should be similar.

The point of earn–burn analytics is to predict when customers will earn, how much they'll earn, and how sensitive they are to incentives, and then to predict their rewards totals, and when and by how much customers burn through their rewards. Survival modelling (including tobit) are typical examples of techniques to do this.

Checklist

You'll be the smartest person in the room if you:

- [ ] Force your peers to understand that loyalty analytics must be from the customer's, not the firm's, point of view.

- [ ] Realize that earn–burn analysis is key to successful loyalty analytics.

- [ ] Advocate using survival modelling to predict time-until-earn and time-until-burn events.

- [ ] Suggest tobit modelling to predict the amount of earn and the amount of burn events.

IDENTIFYING LOYAL CUSTOMERS   18

MARKETING QUESTION

How do I quantify loyalty? Which customers are transactionally loyal and which are emotionally or brand loyal?

ANALYTIC SOLUTION

Structural equation modelling (SEM)

Structural equation modelling (SEM)

This will unfortunately be a far-too-brief account of SEM. SEM is in the domain of marketing research, rather than direct or database marketing (where we've spent most of our time) but it is so powerful and so fun that a quick tour has to be done.

There are similarities between SEM and simultaneous equations (covered in Chapter 16). They are each about systems of equations. They each deal with endogenous and exogenous variables. They each require the algebraic solution of fixed variables and enough observations to calculate variance. Of course they each require the analyst to think through cause and effect. This is because both techniques are about cause and effect and can be conceptualized as regression equations.

SEM is a marketing research tool while simultaneous equations are an econometric tool. This is the first difference. Another (major) difference is that simultaneous equations are (only) about blatant variables while SEM can contain both blatant as well as latent variables. This is, in my view, the most important (and exciting) difference. Another difference is that simultaneous equations operate on each (raw) observation (say, each row is a customer) but SEM operates on an observation being an element of a covariance matrix. So, with that, let's go on to a few definitions as SEM is a different kind of animal.

FIGURE 18.1   Visual conception

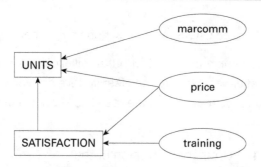

In the contrived Figure 18.1, note that units is CAUSED by marcomm, price and satisfaction. Also see that satisfaction is CAUSED by price and employee training. That is, satisfaction is both a dependent and an independent variable. All of these are blatant (manifest) variables. They can be measured for what they are:

$$\text{Units} = f(\text{price, marcomm, satisfaction})$$
$$\text{Satisfaction} = f(\text{training, price})$$

Examples here will revolve around path analysis. In SAS it will be with proc CALIS.

Let's go over some terminology, as SEM has its own language and jargon. There are two kinds of variables: manifest and latent. Manifest variables are blatant, directly measured, directly observed. These are things like responses, sales, units, price and days between purchase. The second kind of variable is latent. These are (indirectly) estimated through observable data. These are things like satisfaction and loyalty. That is, while there is no quantitative observable metric of satisfaction for example, it can be inferred from observable behaviour.

Now let's mention again exogenous and endogenous variables. Exogenous variables are outside the system; they are independent variables (not caused) but can be either latent or manifest. Endogenous variables are typically (at least) dependent variables and are caused by something else. They also can be either latent or manifest. So, now we're ready to do SEM.

Comparing regression to SEM

For a simple example let's use:

$$\text{proc reg revenue} = f(\text{units, n\_price})$$

and then

$$\text{proc CALIS revenue} = f(\text{units, n\_price})$$

This is a far too simple use of SEM but it will illustrate some important things. Note that all variables are manifest and we have only one equation. Let's say we run proc reg and get the result as shown in Table 18.1.

TABLE 18.1   Ordinary regression output

VARIABLE	PARM ESTIMATE	STANDARD ERROR	T VALUE
Intercept	–8862		
Units	73.24	7.4	9.98
N_Price	111.25	19.03	5.84

Now if we run proc calis (see Table 18.2):

```
proc calis data = xx.xx meanstr;
path
rev <-- units n_price;
run;
```

TABLE 18.2   SEM output

PATH REVENUE	VARIABLE	PARM ESTIMATE	STANDARD ERROR	T VALUE
	Intercept	–8863		
	Units	73.24	1.48	49.39
	N_Price	111.25	2.07	53.81

Proc CALIS gives a lot more (but not shown here) results. The only point here is that SEM and OLS show the same (single equation, manifest) output, in terms of parameter estimates. (The difference in t-value calculation is that regression uses a different denominator for standard error to SEM.)

Calculating impacts

Now let's see what happens when we include more complexity and more realism. Most marketers want to know the impact of their marcomm (and price) on revenue. Assume we did a regression model revenue = f(units, n_price, e-mail, direct mail). (We will ignore the algebraic issue of having both price and units as independent variables, this is for illustrative purposes.) The interest here is marcomm impacts (see Table 18.3).

TABLE 18.3   Single equation with ordinary regression

VARIABLE	PARM ESTIMATE	STANDARD ERROR	T VALUE
Intercept	–9368		
Units	77.08	7.569	9.79
N_Price	115.24	20.112	5.73
E-mail	9.089	2.969	3.06
Direct mail	3.99	1.88	2.12

This indicates that every e-mail sent drives 9.089 in revenue and for every direct mail sent we get 3.99 in revenue. This means that sending 100 each drives 909 and 399 or 1,308 in total revenue. This model implicitly assumes the impact of marcomm is directly on revenue and not on units. The R^2 here is 57%.

Now let's go a step further, and the results will be more interesting. We will use the above path of two equations:

$$\text{Revenue} = f(\text{units, n\_price})$$
$$\text{Units} = f(\text{n\_price, e-mail, direct mail})$$

where marcomm will be number of e-mails and direct mails sent. The hypothesis here is that units and price directly (algebraically in this case) impact revenue. The other hypothesis is that price and marcomm (EM and DM) directly impact units which then indirectly impact revenue. That is, units are both a dependent and an independent variable. That means that revenue comes from both price and units and that units come from price and EM and DM.

The total impact on revenue is shown in Table 18.4.

TABLE 18.4 Simultaneous equation with SEM

PATH REVENUE	VARIABLE	PARM ESTIMATE	STANDARD ERROR	T VALUE
	Intercept	–8863		
	Units	73.24	1.48	49.39
	N_Price	111.25	2.07	53.81
PATH UNITS	Intercept	259		
	N_Price	–2.53	0.082	–30.88
	E-mail	1.266	0.299	4.23
	Direct Mail	1.141	0.089	12.82

Most importantly, note the impact of marcomm is through units, and not to revenue. The impact of 1 e-mail is now 1.266 of revenue and every direct mail is now 1.414. Now sending 100 each only totals 241 in revenue. This is far more realistic than the above model. The R^2 here is 78%. While this is a contrived, overly simplistic model it has complexity that more closely matches reality.

Business case

Scott and his team were facing a difficult deadline. They had to output an SEM loyalty model by the end of the month. They debated over methodology but finally resorted to SEM.

'This is where the real power of SEM comes in,' Scott said, 'the use of latent variables. In this case let's put together a framework for loyalty.'

Note that there is actually no such thing as a blatant entity called or quantified as 'loyalty'. It is a latent variable. The idea is that it is like intelligence, which is also unquantifiable as itself; it can only be indirectly measured as something like a score on an IQ test, which in turn measures dimensions of intelligence: spatial ability, logic, mathematics, verbal skills, and so on. Same is true for loyalty. It can be seen and surmised by other actions.

'So let's use our behavioural segmentation based on customer transactions and responses to marcomm. We are interested in how loyal each segment is, which is not necessarily the same thing as how much they spend or how many transactions they have. So we do primary marketing research and ask questions about opinions and attitudes around price, value, quality and satisfaction. These metrics will show a range of loyalty. We also ask about share of voice, competitive density and the convenience of our stores compared to our competitors.' Scott sketched the below framework on the white board.

The model in Figure 18.2 tries to put a framework together that says consumer behaviour (transactions, responses, etc) is caused by a spectrum of loyalty (from none to transactional to emotional) which are in turn caused by attitudes around price, value, satisfaction and quality as well as opinions/metrics of operational logistics like convenience, share of voice and competitive density.

FIGURE 18.2   Loyalty framework

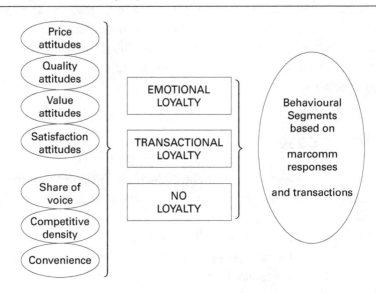

So the general analytic idea is that there are no such metrics or quantities as emotional or transactional loyalty. These are latent variables. But adding these variables helps explain the behaviour of customers purchasing and customers responding. This latent variable is discovered by a factor analysis-type technique used in SEM. That is, the manifest variables indirectly show the influence of the latent variable and that latent variable is 'teased out' and labelled.

(A quick note about the difference between transactional and emotional loyalty should clarify this important point. It is possible for a customer to appear very loyal in terms of buying a lot of products, having a short time between purchases, or responding to marcomm, but not be in fact actually very loyal. These are heavy purchasers because there might not be any competitors around, or our stores are very convenient or our share of voice is comparatively large. Thus it's important to know how 'loyal' customers are, independent of other dimensions. That is, transactionally loyal customers may jump ship if competitors move in near their location, or change their share of voice.)

A couple of weeks later his team had an output. The results shown below are from applying the loyalty model to two different segments, say X and Y. The segments were defined by (transactions and marcomm response) behaviour. The question is how loyal (what kind of loyalty) they are and what can be done about it. Let's say that each segment has generally the same metrics on transactions and responses. Segment X scores as a transactionally loyal customer. Note the parameter estimates of convenience and competitive density are very high and significant while share of voice is strong and negative. These are traditional indications of the transactionally loyal segment. Note also high and positive impacts of attitudes around price and quality. And recognize that most of the variables on the emotional path are insignificant.

TABLE 18.5   Segment X, transactional loyalty

path transactional	variable	parm est	st error	t value
	price	5.65	3.23	1.75
	quality	6.21	1.65	3.75
	value	3.03	2.07	1.47
	satisfaction	1.35	0.66	2.05
	convenience	5.22	0.75	6.96
	competition	2.66	0.99	2.68
	share of voice	−1.55	1.03	−1.51

path emotional	variable	parm est	st error	t value
	price	0.03	2.66	0.01
	quality	0.56	1.07	0.53
	value	1.04	2.36	0.44
	satisfaction	1.66	1.03	1.62
	convenience	1.99	1.66	1.2
	competition	0.66	2.04	0.32
	share of voice	2.55	1.69	1.51

Now, a segment that scores as a strong transactionally loyal only segment is something of a red flag. This is especially true if they LOOK like they are loyal based on their number and amount of purchases.

How can we use the above model to move the segment from mere transactionally loyal to emotionally loyal? The answer is in the emotional loyal path. The single largest impact is share of voice and that is a metric we can (somewhat) control. There is a business case around what is the cost to spend and increase our relative share of voice applied against the added security (and perhaps increased purchasing) of a segment that evolves into emotionally loyal. See that share of voice is negative in the transactional path? As SOV increases this segment is less transactionally and more emotionally loyal.

Now let's look at the opposite kind of loyalty, the brand or emotional kind. These are customers that love our brand, no matter what. View the output shown in Table 18.6 for segment Y, which scores mostly as an emotionally loyal group. Note on the emotional path convenience and competitive density are negative. This segment is so connected to the brand that even if it is inconvenient to go to our store they go anyway and even if more competition moves in these customers come to our store anyway. This is emotional loyalty. You see also that on the emotional path, while price is positive it's insignificant and quality is very small. It should be no surprise that both value and satisfaction are high. On the transactional path none of those metrics are significant.

This is the power of SEM, hypothesizing and testing a latent variable. This latent variable accounts for movement in the customer transactions and customer responses. If only a blatant or manifest model was used the fit would not have been so well and the insights (differentiating between the two kinds of loyalty) would not be realized. So is that cool, or what?

TABLE 18.6   Segment Y, emotional loyalty

path transactional	variable	parm est	st error	t value
	price	−1.27	5.65	−0.22
	quality	2.07	6.24	0.33
	value	2.07	1.65	1.25
	satisfaction	0.03	5.07	0.01
	convenience	0.23	0.2	1.17
	competition	0.04	0.02	1.8
	share of voice	−2.65	1.54	−1.72
path emotional	**variable**	**parm est**	**st error**	**t value**
	price	3.25	3.04	1.07
	quality	0.24	0.12	2.06
	value	1.26	0.76	1.67
	satisfaction	3.23	1.23	2.63
	convenience	−3.65	1.26	−2.91
	competition	−2.07	0.56	−3.66
	share of voice	1.27	0.87	1.45

Conclusion

Structural equation modelling (SEM) is a powerful systems method especially in dealing with latent variables. This has great importance into subjects like satisfaction in terms of loyalty and quantifying various degrees of loyalty.

Checklist

You'll be the smartest person in the room if you:

☐ Differentiate between structural equation models (SEM) and simultaneous equations. SEM and simultaneous equations are both systems of equations, but SEM can measure and quantify both blatant and latent variables.

☐ Argue that the power of SEM is in uncovering latent variables.

INTRODUCTION TO SEGMENTATION   19

MARKETING QUESTION

What do I need to know about analytics in order to understand my customer market? What is the approach or philosophy used to understand my customer market?

ANALYTIC SOLUTION

Introduction to segmentation

Overview

As mentioned earlier, there are two general types of multivariate analysis: dependent variable techniques and interrelationship techniques. The point of dependent variable techniques is to understand to what extent the dependent variable depends on the independent variables. That is, how does price impact units, where units is the dependent variable (something we are trying to understand or explain) and price is the independent variable, a variable that is hypothesized to cause the movement in the dependent variable. Interrelationship techniques have a completely different point of view. These include multivariate algorithms like factor analysis, segmentation, and multidimensional scaling. Interrelationship techniques are trying to understand how variables (price, product purchases, advertising spend, etc) interact (interrelate) together. Remember how factor analysis was used to correct for collinearity in regression? It did this by extracting the variance of the independent variables in such a way that each factor (which contained the variables) was uncorrelated with all other factors, that is, the interrelationship between the independent variables was constructed to form factors.

This section will spend considerable effort on an interrelationship technique that is of utmost interest and importance to marketing: segmentation.

Introduction to segmentation

OK. This introductory chapter is designed to detail some of the strategic uses and necessities of segmentation. The chapter following this will dive into more of the analytic techniques and what segmentation output may look like. Segmentation is often the biggest analytic project available and one that provides potentially more strategic insights than any other.

What is segmentation? What is a segment?

A good place to start is to make sure we know what we're talking about. Radical, I know. By definition, segmentation is a process of taxonomy, a way to divide something into parts, a way to separate a market into sub-markets. It can be called 'clustering' or 'partitioning'. Thus, a market segment (cluster) is a sub-set of the market (or customer market, or database).

The general definition of a segment is that members of the segment are 'homogeneous within and heterogeneous between'. That means that a good segmentation solution will have all the members (say, customers) within a segment to be very similar to each other but very dissimilar to all members of all other segments. Homogeneous means 'same' and heterogeneous means 'different'.

It's possible to have very advanced statistical algorithms to accomplish this, or it can be a very crude business rule. Note that a business rule could simply be, 'Separate the database into four parts: highest use, medium use, low use and no use of our product'. This managerial fiat has been (and still is) used by many companies.

RFM (recency, frequency and monetary variables) is another simple business rule: separate the database into, say, deciles based on three metrics: how recently a customer purchased, how frequently a customer purchased and how much money a customer spent. Many companies are not doing much more than this, in terms of segmentation. These companies are certainly not marketing companies because techniques like RFM are really from a financial, and not a customer, point of view. Therefore, a segment is that entity wherein all members assigned to that segment are, by some definition, alike. More on this later.

Strategic uses of segmentation

So, why segment at all? There are three typical uses of segmentation: finding similar members, making modelling better and – most important – using marketing strategy to attack each segment differently.

Finding homogeneous members is a valuable use of a statistical technique. The business problem tends to be: find all those that are 'alike' and see how, say, satisfaction differs between them, or find all those that are 'homogeneous' by some measure and see how usage varies between them.

A simple example might be in telecoms, where we are looking at churn (attrition) rates. We want to understand the motivation of churn, what behaviour can predict churn. So, conduct segmentation and identify customers in each segment that are alike in all important ways to the business (products, usage, demographics, channel preferences, etc) and show different churn rates by segment. Note that churn is not the variable that all segments are alike on; churn is what we are trying to understand. Thus we control for several influences (all members within a segment are alike) and now can see high vs. low churners, after all other significant variables have been eliminated.

A second usage, also sophisticated and nuanced, is to use segmentation to improve modelling. In the above churn example, say segmentation was done and we want to predict churn. We run a separate regression model for each segment and find that different independent variables affect churn differently. This will be far more accurate (and actionable) than one (average) model applied to everyone without segmentation. This approach takes advantage of the different reasons to churn. One segment might churn due to dropped calls, another might churn because of the price of the plan and another is sensitive to their bill based on calls, minutes and data used. Thus, each model will exploit these differences and be far more accurate than otherwise. The more accurate the model, the greater the insights; the greater the understanding, the more obvious the strategy of how to combat churn in each segment.

But from a marketing point of view, the reason to segment is the simple answer that not everyone is alike, not all customers are the same. One size does not fit all.

I'd even offer a tweak on 'segmentation' at this point. Market segmentation should use the marketing concept, where the customer is king and strategy is therefore customer-centric. Note that an algorithm like RFM is from the firm's (financial) point of view with metrics that are important to the firm. RFM is about designing value tiers based on a financial perspective.

Since marketing segmentation should be from the customer's point of view, why do segmentation? That is, how does 'one size NOT fit all' operate in terms of customer-centricity?

Generally, it's based on recognizing that different customers have different sensitivities. These different sensitivities cause them to behave differently because they are motivated differently. That is, they are sensitive to different things.

This means considerable effort needs to be applied to learn what makes each behavioural segment a segment. It means developing a strategy to exploit these different sensitivities and motivations.

Usually there is a segment sensitive to price, and a segment not sensitive to price. Often there is a segment that prefers one channel (say, online) and a segment that prefers another channel (say, offline). Typically, one segment will have high penetration of product X while another segment will have high penetration of product Y. One segment needs to be communicated with differently (style, imaging, messaging) to another segment. Note that this is far more involved than a simple business rule.

The idea is that if a segment is sensitive to, say, price, then those members should get a discount or a better offer, in order to maximize their probability to purchase. (They face an elastic demand curve.) The segment that is not sensitive to price (because they are loyal, wealthy, or perhaps with no substitutes available) should not be given the discount because they don't need it in order to purchase.

I know the above adds complexity to the analysis. But note that consumer behaviour IS complex. Behaviour incorporates simultaneous motivations and multidimensional factors, sometimes nearly irrational. Understanding consumer behaviour requires a complex, sophisticated solution, if the goal is to do marketing, if the goal is to be customer-centric. A simpler solution won't work. Much like the problem that happens when we take a 3-dimensional globe of the earth and spread it out over a two-dimensional space. Greenland is now way off in size; the world is wrong. Being overly simplistic produces wrong results, just like applying a univariate solution to a multivariate problem will produce wrong results.

A priori or not?

As a practitioner's guide to marketing science, it should come as no surprise that I advocate statistical analysis to perform segmentation. However, it's a fact that sometimes there are (top–down) dictums that define segments. These are managerial fiats that demand a market be based (a priori) on managerial judgement, rather than some analytic technique. The usual dimension(s) by which managers want to artificially define their market tend to be usage, profit, satisfaction, size, and growth. Analytically, this is a univariate approach to what is clearly a multivariate problem.

In my opinion, there is a place for managerial judgement, but it is NOT in segment definition. After the segments are defined, then managerial judgement should ascertain if the solution makes sense, if the segments themselves are actionable.

Conceptual process

Settle on a (marketing or customer) strategy

The general first step in behavioural segmentation is one of strategy. After the firm establishes goals, a strategy needs to be in place to reach those goals. There should be a champion, a business leader, a stakeholder who is the ultimate user of the segmentation.

Analytics needs to recognize that a segmentation not driven by strategy is akin to a body without a skeleton. Strategy supports everything. A very different segmentation should result if the strategy is about market share as opposed to a strategy about net margin.

A strategy discussion should revolve around customer behaviour. What is the mindset in a customer's mind, what is the behaviour we are trying to understand, what incentive are we employing? Any good segmentation solution should tie together customer behaviour and marketing strategy. Remember, marketing is customer-centric.

Collect appropriate (behavioural) data

The next analytic step in behavioural segmentation is to collect appropriate (behavioural) data. This tends to be generally around transactions (purchases) and marcomm responses.

A few comments ought to be made about what is meant by 'behavioural data'. My theory of consumer behaviour (and it's OK if you don't agree) is to envision four levels (see Figure 19.1): primary motivations, experiential motivations, behaviours and results.

Results (typically financial) are caused by behaviours (usually some kind of transactions/purchases and marcomm responses), which are caused by one or both (primary and experiential) motivations. Primary motivations (price valuation, attitudes about lifestyle, tastes and preferences, etc) are generally psychographic and not really seen. They are motivational causes (searching, need arousal, etc) without brand interaction. Experiential motivations tend to have brand interaction and are other motivators to additional behaviours that ultimately cause (financial) results. These motivations are things like loyalty, engagement and satisfaction. Note that engagement is an experiential cause (there has been interaction with the brand) and is not a behaviour. Engagement would be metrics like recency and frequency. More will be said on this topic in discussing RFM later. I'll warn you this is one of my soap boxes.

FIGURE 19.1   Motivations causing results

REVENUE

growth   *margin*   RESULTS

LTV

PURCHASES

VISITS   usage   *Product Penetration*   BEHAVIOURS

responses

usage

SATISFACTION   *engage-*   EXPERIENTIAL

Loyalty   *ment*   MOTIVATIONS

VELOCITY   *lifestyle*

ATTITUDES   **Price**   Channel preference   PRIMARY

tastes and preferences   *SEARCHING*   MOTIVATIONS

promotions

NEED AROUSAL

Usually transactions and marcomm responses (eg from direct mail, e-mail) are the main dimensions of behavioural segmentation. Often additional variables are created from these dimensions.

We want to know, for example, how many times a customer purchased, how much each time, what products were purchased, what categories each product purchased belongs to. Often valuable profiling variables go along with this, including net margin on each purchase, cost of goods sold, etc. We want to know the number of transactions over a period of time, the number of units and if any discounts were applied to these transactions.

In terms of marcomm responses we want to collect data on the kind of vehicle (direct mail, e-mail), opens, clicks, website visits, store purchases involving discounts used. We want to know when each vehicle was sent and what category of product was featured on each vehicle. Any versioning needs to be collected, and any offers/promotions need to be annotated in the database. All of this data surrounding transactions and responses is the basis of customer behaviour.

Generally, we expect to find a segment that is heavily penetrated in one type of category (broad products purchased) but not another and this will be different by more than one segment. As bears repeating, one segment is heavily penetrated by category X, while another is heavily penetrated by category Y. We also expect to find one or more segments that prefer e-mail or online but not direct mail, or vice versa. We typically find a segment that is sensitive to price and one that is not sensitive to price. These insights come differently from these behavioural dimensions.

Create or use additional data

Now comes the fun part. Here you can create additional data. This data at least takes the form of seasonality variables, calculates time between each purchase, time between categories purchased, peaks and valleys of transactions and units and revenue, share of categories (eg percentage of baby products compared to total, percentage of entertainment categories compared to total) etc. There should be metrics such as number of units and transactions per customer, percentage of discounts per customer, and top two or three categories purchased per customer. All of these can be used/tested in the segmentation.

As for marcomm, there should be a host of metrics around marcomm type and offer and time until purchase. There should be business rules tying a campaign to a purchase. There should be variables indicating categories featured on the cover, or subject lines, or offers and promotions.

Note how all of the above expand behavioural data. But there are other sources of data as well. Often primary marketing research is used. This tends to be around satisfaction or loyalty, something about competitive substitutes, maybe marcomm awareness or importance of each marcomm vehicle.

Third-party overlay data are rich sources of additional insights into fleshing out the segments. This is often matched data like demographics, interests, attitudes or lifestyles. This data is typically most helpful when it deals with attitudes or lifestyle, but demographics can be interesting as well. Again all of this additional data is about fleshing out the segments, and trying to understand the mindset/rationale of each segment.

Run the algorithm

As mentioned previously, the algorithm discussion will be covered in depth in the next chapter, but a few comments can be made now, particularly in terms of process. Note that the algorithm is guided by strategy and uses (defining or segmenting) variables based on strategy.

The algorithm is the analytic guts of segmentation and care should be taken in choosing which technique to use. The algorithm should be fast and non-arbitrary. Analytically, we are trying to achieve maximum separation (segment distinctiveness).

The ultimate idea of segmentation is to level a different strategy against each segment. Therefore, each segment should have a different reason for BEING a segment.

The algorithm needs to provide diagnostics to guide optimization. The general metric of success is 'homogeneous within and heterogeneous between' segments. There have been many such metrics offered (eg in SAS, proc discrim uses 'the logarithm of the determinant of the covariance matrix' as a metric of success).

In the profiling, the differentiation of each segment should make itself clear. Just to stack the deck, let me define what a good algorithm for segmentation should be. It should be multivariable, multivariate and probabilistic. It should be multivariable because consumer behaviour is most certainly explained by more than one variable, it should be multivariate because these variables are impacting consumer behaviour simultaneously, interacting with each other. It should be probabilistic because consumer behaviour is probabilistic; it has a distribution and at some point that behaviour can even be irrational.

Profile the output

Profiling is what we show to other people to prove the solution does discriminate between segments. Generally, the means and/or frequencies of each key variable (especially transactions and marcomm responses) are shown to quickly gauge differences by each segment. Note that the more distinct each segment is the more obvious a strategy (for each segment) becomes.

Showing the means of key performance indicators (KPIs) by segment is common, but often another metric teases out differences more effectively. Using indexes often speeds distinctiveness. That is, take each segment's mean and divide by the total mean. For example, segment 1 has average revenue of 1,500 and segment 2 has average revenue of 750 and the total average (all segments together) is 1,000. Dividing segment 1 by the total is 1,500 / 1,000 = 1.5, ie segment 1 has revenue 50% above average.

Note also that segment 2 is 750 / 1,000 = 0.75 meaning that segment 2 contributes revenue 25% less than average. Applying indices to all metrics by segment immediately shows differences. This is especially obvious where small numbers are concerned.

As another example, say segment 1 has a response rate of 1.9% and the overall grand total response rate is 1.5%. While comparing these numbers (segment 1 to total) is only 0.4% different, note that the index of segment 1 / total is 1.9% / 1.5% showing that segment 1 is 27% greater than average. This is why we like to (and should) use indices.

While seeing drastic difference in each segment is very satisfying, the most enjoyable part of profiling often is the NAMING of each segment. First you must realize that naming a segment helps distinguish the segments. The more segments you have the more important this becomes.

I have a couple of suggestions about naming segments; take them as you see fit. Sometimes the naming of segments is left to the creative department and that's OK. But usually analytics has to come up with the names.

Each name should be only two or three words, if possible. They should be more informative than something like 'high revenue segment' or 'low response segment'. They should incorporate two or three similar dimensions. Either keep most of them to product/marcomm response dimensions, or keep them along a strategic dimension or two (high growth, cost to serve, net margin, etc). It's tempting to name them playfully but this still has to be usable. So, while 'Bohemian Mix' is fun, what does it mean strategically or from a marketing point of view?

Model to score database (if from a sample)

The next step, if the segmentation has been done on a sample, is to score the database with each customer's probability to belong to each segment. This is often carried out quickly with discriminate analysis. Apply (in SAS) proc discrim to the sample and get the equations that score each customer into a segment. (Discriminate analysis is a common technique, once categories (segments) are defined, to fit variables in equations to predict category (segment) membership.) Then run these equations against the database.

If this is accurate enough, then you're set. But sometimes discrim isn't accurate enough. I myself think this is because you have to use the same variables (although with different weights) on each segment. This can be inefficient. There is also the assumption inherent in discrim about the same variance across a segment which is hardly ever true, so you may need to turn to another technique.

I have often settled for logistic regression, where a different equation scores each segment. That is, if I have five segments, the first logit will be with a binary dependent variable: 1 if the customer is in segment 1 and 0 if not. The second logit will be a 1 if the customer is in segment 2 and a 0 if not. Then I put in variables to maximize probability of each segment and I remove those variables that are insignificant and run all equations against all customers. Each customer will have a probability to belong to each segment and the max score wins, ie the segment that has the highest probability is the segment to which the customer is assigned.

Test and learn

The typical last step is to create a test and learn plan. This is generally a broad-based test design, aimed at learning which elements drive results. This is directly informed by the segmentation insights.

The overall idea here is to develop a testing plan to take advantage of segmentation. The first thing to test is typically selection/targeting. Pull a sample of those likely to belong to a very highly profitable, heavy usage segment and do a mailing to them and compare revenue and responses to some general control group. These high-end segments should drastically outperform the business-as-usual (BAU) group.

A common next step (depending on strategy) might be promotional testing. This would usually follow with elasticity modelling by segment. Often one or more segments are found to be insensitive to price and one or more segments are found to be sensitive to price. The test here is to offer promotions and determine if the segment insensitive to price will still purchase even with a lower discount. This means the firm does not have to give away margin to get the same amount of purchases.

Other typical tests revolve around product categories, channel preference and messaging. A full factorial design could get much learning immediately and then marcomm could be aimed appropriately. The general idea is that if a segment is, say, heavily penetrated in product X, send them a product X message. If a segment might have a propensity for product Y (given product X) do a test and see how to incentivize broader category purchases. The next chapter will go through a detailed example of what this testing might mean.

Conclusion

Segmentation is a very powerful and common marketing analytics technique. While it is often thought of as strictly an analytic exercise, it becomes lucrative if put in a strategy process. That is, have segmentation as a strategic point of view. So the first step in segmentation should be a strategic exercise.

I advocate a behavioural segmentation (especially in terms of customer analytics) based on behaviours tracked from transactions and marcomm responses. The idea is that segments rooted in behaviour do not change much. Thus, if a customer is sensitive to price then they will always be sensitive to price (unless they win the lottery). If a customer prefers online as a shopping channel they will tend to always prefer online shopping. If a segment has a deep penetration of product X, then they will always have an affinity for that product.

This is why behavioural segmentation is so powerful: each segment is sensitive to a different marketing mix which allows a unique strategy. This portfolio approach means that marketers have a lot of testing options: different discounts, different marcomm vehicles, different shopping and purchasing channels and different product mixes and bundling strategies.

Checklist

You'll be the smartest person in the room if you:

☐ Point out that segmentation is a strategic, not an analytic, exercise.

☐ Remember that segmentation is mostly a marketing construct.

☐ Argue that segmentation is about what's important to a consumer, not what's important to a firm.

☐ Recall that segmentation gives insights into marketing research, marketing strategy, marketing communications and marketing economics.

☐ Observe the 4Ps of strategic marketing: partition, probe, prioritize and position.

☐ Uncompromisingly demand that RFM be viewed as a service to the firm, not a service to the consumer.

☐ Require each segment to have its own story and rationale for WHY it is a segment. There should be a different strategy levelled at each segment, otherwise there is no point in being a segment.

TOOLS FOR SUCCESSFUL SEGMENTATION

20

MARKETING QUESTION

What analytic tools and techniques are used to do segmentation?

ANALYTIC SOLUTION

Overview of general segmentation algorithms

Overview

The previous chapter was meant to be a general/strategic overview of segmentation. This chapter is designed to show the analytic aspects of it, which is the heart of the segmentation process. Analytics is the fulcrum of the whole project.

Metrics of successful segmentation

As mentioned in Chapter 19, the general idea of successful segmentation is 'homogeneous within and heterogeneous between'. There are several possible approaches to quantifying this goal. Generally, a ratio of those members in the segment is compared to all those members not in the segment and the smaller the better. This helps us to compare a 3-segment solution with a 4-segment solution, or a 4-segment solution using variables a–f with a 4-segment solution using variables d–j. SAS (via proc discrim) has the 'log of the determinant of the covariant matrix'. This is a good metric to use in comparing solutions even if it's a badly-named metric.

General analytic techniques

Business rules

There may be a place for business-rule segmentation. If data is sparse, under-populated, or very few dimensions are available, there's little point trying to do an analytic segmentation. There's nothing for the algorithm to operate on.

I (again) caution against a managerial fiat. I have had managers who invested themselves in the segmentation design. They have told me how to define the segments. This is typically flawed. I wouldn't say ignore management's knowledge or intuition of their market and their customers. My advice is to go through the segmentation process, do the analytics and see what the results look like. Typically, the analytic results are appealing and more compelling than managerial judgement. This is because a manager's dictum is around one or two or at most three dimensions, arbitrarily defined. But the analytic output optimizes the variables and separation is the mathematical 'best'. It would be unlikely that one person's intuition could outperform a statistical algorithm. I would even say that if an analytic output is very different to a manager's point of view, that manager has a lot to learn about his own market. The statistical algorithm encourages learning. Most often managerial fiat is about usage (high, medium and low), satisfaction, net profit, etc. None of these require or allow much investigation into WHY the results are what they are.

A good overview of segmentation, from the managerial role and not the analytical role, is Art Weinstein's book, *Market Segmentation*. That book provides a good discussion of segmentation based on business rules.

Note that RFM is covered in specific detail in Chapter 23.

CHAID

CHAID (chi-squared automatic interaction detection) is an improvement over AID (automatic interaction detection). Strictly speaking, CHAID is a dependent-variable technique, NOT an interrelationship technique. I'm including it here because CHAID is often used as a segmentation solution.

This brings us to the question, 'Why use a dependent-variable technique to do segmentation?' My answer is that it is inappropriate. A dependent-variable technique is designed to understand (predict) what causes a dependent variable to move. By definition, segmentation is not about explaining the movement in some dependent variable.

So, how does it work? While there are many variations of the algorithm, in general it works in the following way. CHAID takes the dependent variable and looks at the independent variables and finds the one independent variable that 'splits' the dependent variable best. 'Best' here is per the chi-squared test. (AID was based on the F-test.) It then takes that (2nd-level) variable and searches the remaining independent variables to test which one best splits that 2nd-level variable. It does this until the number of levels assigned is reached, or until there is no improvement in convergence.

Figure 20.1 is a simple example. Product revenue is the dependent variable and CHAID is run and the best split is found to be income. Income is split into two groups, high income and low income. The next best variable is response rate, where each income level has two different response rates. High income is split in terms of response rate > 9% and response rate > 6% and < 9%. Low income is split between < 2% and > 2% and < 6%. Thus, this simplified example would show four segments: high income/high response, high income/medium response, low income/medium response and low income/low response.

The advantages of CHAID are that it is simple and easy to use and easy to explain. It provides a stunning visual to show how to interpret its output.

The disadvantages are many. First, it is not a model in the statistical/ mathematical sense of the word, but a heuristic, a guide. This means the analysis tends to be unstable, ie different samples can produce wildly different results. There are no coefficients that show significance, there are no signs on the variables (positive or negative) and there is no real measure of fit.

FIGURE 20.1   CHAID example

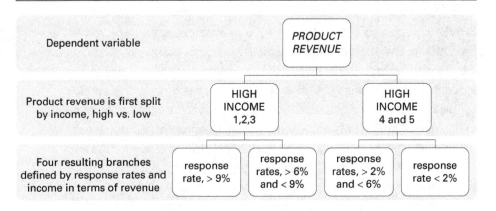

CHAID is a popular technique, due to its ease and simplicity. I would suggest it is not appropriate for segmentation. Its best use is probably in terms of data exploration.

Hierarchical clustering

Hierarchical clustering IS an interrelationship technique. It also has a graphical display but unlike CHAID it is NOT visually appealing.

Hierarchical clustering calculates a 'nearness metric', a type of similarity via some interrelationship variables. There are many options how to do this but conceptually the idea is that some observations (say customers) are 'close to each other' based on some similar variables. Then a dendrogram (a horizontal tree structure) is produced and the analyst chooses how to divide the resultant graphics (see Figure 20.2).

Note that, for instance, observations 34 and 56 are joined together (because they are similar) and these are next joined to observation 111. Now there are three observations in this cluster. As the number of observations increases, the graphic is less and less usable. One disadvantage is

FIGURE 20.2 Hierarchical clustering example

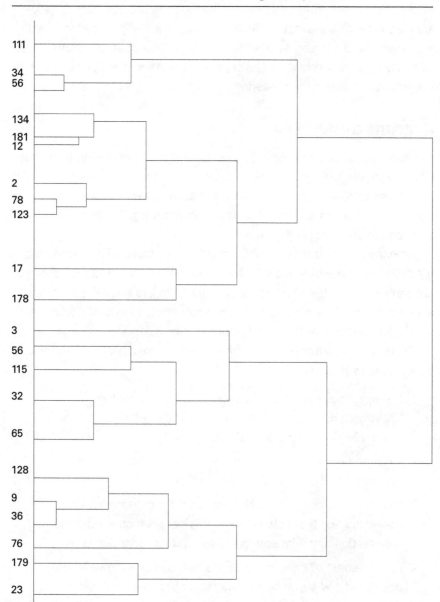

that the analyst is required to (arbitrarily) decide where to break the clusters off. It is therefore ultimately up to the analyst to choose how many and which observations are in the final clusters. Arbitrary choice is NOT based on analytics, but intuition.

An advantage of hierarchical clustering is that it calculates the distance of every observation from all other observations, so the starting 'seeds' are mathematically distinct. Often hierarchical clustering is used for nothing else than these starting seeds as an input into another algorithm. Note James Myers' book on segmentation, which has a very good and conceptual treatment of hierarchical clustering.

K-means clustering

K-means is probably the most popular (analytic) segmentation technique. SAS (using proc fastclus) and SPSS (using partitioning) have very powerful algorithms to do K-means clustering. K-means is easy to do, fairly easy to understand and explain and the output is compelling. K-means works and has been in use for over 50 years.

K-means was invented by zoologists in the 1960s for phylum classification. It's called K-means because K is the number of clusters and the centroids are the means of the clusters. They were trying to decide, based on an animal's (particularly a butterfly's) characteristics, to which phylum they belonged to. They wanted an algorithm for taxonomy.

The general algorithm (and as with all other techniques, there are various versions) is as follows:

1 Set up: choose number of clusters, choose some kind of 'maximum distance' to define cluster membership and choose which clustering variables to use.

2 Find the first observation that has all the clustering variables populated and call this cluster 1.

3 Find the next observation that has all the clustering variables populated and test how far away this observation is from the first observation. If it's far enough away, then call this cluster 2.

4 Find the next observation that has all the clustering variables populated and test how far away this observation is from the first and second observations (clusters). If it's far enough away, then call this cluster 3. Continue with Steps 2–4 until the number of clusters chosen is defined.

5 Go to the next observation and test which cluster it is closest to and assign that observation to that cluster.

6 Continue with Step 5 until all observations that have the clustering variables populated have been assigned.

There are several things good about this algorithm. It is very fast and can handle a large amount of data. It works. It will achieve some kind of separation.

There are many disadvantages. Personally, I hate the arbitrariness of what the analyst must decide. As stated above, the analyst tells the algorithm how many clusters to form (as if she knows). There is little (analytically) on which to base this important criterion. Second, the analyst has to tell the algorithm what variables to use to define the clusters. Again, as if she knows. This is an extremely important choice. The clusters are DEFINED based on this arbitrary decision.

Another disadvantage with K-means is that there are no real diagnostics on how well it fits, how well it predicts, how well it scores those observations (customers) into each segment. Because it's based on the square root of Euclidean distance:

$$\sqrt{\frac{(X2 - X1)}{(Y2 - Y1)}}$$

each observation is placed in the segment it is 'closest to'. There is no likelihood metric. Suppose a customer is new on file, or has some unusual behaviour, this customer might not demonstrate a particular segment behaviour but is still placed somewhere, regardless.

Because of these arbitrary choices (and the fact that K-means gives no diagnostics to aid these choices) most clustering projects end up with the analyst generating many solutions. He will do a 4- and a 5- and 6- and a 7- and an 8-cluster solution. He will use in each of the variables 1–5 and then variables 5–10 and then variables 2–12, etc. Because there are no real diagnostics to guide him he will output reams of paper and share these piles of profiles with his peers and the ultimate users of the segmentation and basically throw up his hands and say, 'What do you think? Which of these 20 outputs do you like the best?' And then maybe somebody will decide what they like, typically for strategic reasons. Note the subjectivity.

Another obvious disadvantage (given the algorithm above) is that if, say, the order of the data-set is different, the K-means solution will be different. Some algorithms improve this option by not just going down the list, but taking a random observation as each starting seed. This is better, but the same problem remains. Re-order, or re-do, the algorithm – with the same number of clusters and the same variables – and the output will be (very) different. This should strike all analytics people as a great problem.

A last problem with K-means is that it is not an optimizing algorithm. It does not maximize or minimize anything. It has no generally controlling objective. It is mathematic, not statistic.

Therefore, I would suggest that K-means is not a viable option for actionable segmentation. The algorithm is too arbitrary and the output is subjective, something most good analysts abhor.

Latent class analysis

Latent class analysis (LCA) is a massive improvement over all the above. It is now the state-of-the-art in segmentation. To me, the best software for this is Latent Gold from Statistical Innovations. Jay Magdison has written some of the best articles on it. Especially see the ones called 'LCA, a Gentle, Non-technical Introduction' and 'LCA Compared to K-means'.

LCA takes a completely different view of segmentation. Rather than, as in the case of K-means where the variables define the segments, LCA assumes the scores on the variables are caused by the (hidden) segment. That is, LCA posits a latent (categorical) variable (segment membership) that maximizes the likelihood of observing the scores seen on the variables.

It then runs this taxonomy and creates a probability of each observation belonging to each segment. The segment that has the highest probability is the segment into which the observation is placed. This means LCA is a statistical technique and not a mathematical (like hierarchical or K-means clustering) technique.

There are some disadvantages of LCA. SAS does not do it, at least not as a proc. SPSS does not do it either. You have to buy special software. Statistical Innovations created Latent Gold which has probably become the gold standard (get it, 'gold'?). It also requires some training and some expertise in order to do it, but Latent Gold is menu-driven and very easy to use. Also, like the light bulb, it is not true that you have to understand all of the intricate details in order to use it. Some training is required, but the results are well worth it.

The advantages have been alluded to but just to be clear: LCA has a LOT of advantages. Ultimately segmentation's usefulness is about strategy. The better the distinctiveness the more obviously a strategy becomes levelled on each segment.

However, there are several important analytic advantages, especially in the way Latent Gold articulates the algorithm. First, LCA tells you the optimal number of segments. You do not have to guess. LCA uses the BIC (Bayes Information Criterion) and −LL (negative log likelihood) and error rate to give you diagnostics as to what is the 'best' number of segments given these scores on these variables and this data-set.

Second, LCA gives indications as to which variables are significant in the segmentation solution. You do not have to guess. Any variable that has an R^2 < 10% can be deemed insignificant.

Third, LCA produces an output that scores every observation with the probability of belonging to each segment. If observation # 1 has a probability of belonging to segment 1 of 95% and probability of belonging to segment 2 of 5% it's pretty obvious to which segment that observation belongs. Observation # 1 exhibits very strong segment 1 behaviour. But what about observation #2 that has a probability of belonging to segment 1 of 55% and probability of belonging to segment 2 of 45%? This observation does not demonstrate very strong segment behaviour, for any segment. Under K-means this observation would likely be assigned to segment 1. But LCA gives you a diagnostic. Typically, some assumption should be made. It's usually something like, 'any observation that does not score at least 70% likelihood of belonging to any segment be eliminated from the output'. Those observations are placed in some other bucket to be dealt with in some other way. There should not be more than 5% of these outliers, given most marketing models are at 95% confidence. A good solution will have far less than 5% outliers.

These diagnostics make the analytics very fast and very clean. It also makes the segmentation solution very distinct. As mentioned, this is the hallmark of a good segmentation solution: distinctiveness. But this is not just valuable for the analyst; it is of utmost importance to the strategist. The more distinct the segmentation solution is the clearer each strategy becomes.

Table 20.1 shows where several segmentation algorithms go well in terms of segmentation options. Note that only LCA checks all four boxes.

TABLE 20.1   Segmentation algorithms compared

	RFM	CHAID	KMeans	LCA
MULTIVARIABLE	XX	XX	XX	XX
CUST-CENTRIC				XX
MULTIVARIATE			XX	XX
PROBABILISTIC				XX

Conclusion

Strictly speaking, there are a lot of ways to do segmentation. The concept of segmentation is just a way to divide the database into sub-sections. The overall idea is 'homogeneous within and heterogeneous between'. This means a successful segmentation will be one wherein the members assigned to a segment are all very similar (based on some measure of similarity) and by definition are very dissimilar (based on whatever definition of dissimilarity is deemed useful) to all other members in other segments.

This sub-division can happen with simple or complex rules or algorithms. A business rule that just sorts customers by historically high vs. medium vs. low usage is a kind of segmentation that uses just one dimension. And there are mathematically and statistically sophisticated algorithms that can simultaneously optimize many dimensions, eg latent class analysis.

So the choice of algorithm depends on data and timing and strategy and expertise. This chapter was meant to give a generalized view of common potential algorithms.

Checklist

You'll be the smartest person in the room if you:

☐ Remember SAS (in proc discrim) gives a metric of an optimal segmentation solution as the 'log of the determinant of the covariant matrix'.

☐ Recall the variety of segmentation techniques: business rules, CHAID, hierarchical clustering, K-means, latent class analysis (LCA), etc.

☐ Point out that LCA provides the optimal number of segments, diagnoses which variables are significant and calculates a probability score for every member belonging to every segment – nothing is arbitrary.

☐ Use the behavioural segmentation process: strategize, collect behavioural data, create/use additional data, run the chosen algorithm and profile segment output.

DRAWING INSIGHTS 21
FROM SEGMENTATION

MARKETING QUESTION

What kind of insights can segmentation provide? How is segmentation used strategically?

ANALYTIC SOLUTION

Segmentation example

Business case

Scott's boss Becky called him into her office. He waited for her to take a sip of coffee and sigh.

'So Scott,' she said. 'We are ready to make a major push in customer strategy. We've used so much of what your group has done this last year. We want to take it to the next level.'

'That sounds good. What does that mean for my team?'

'We'd like to explore versioning our direct mail catalogues, positioning our e-mails more strategically, and so on. We all remember your ONE SIZE DOES NOT FIT ALL speech at the offsite last quarter. It's spot on. We're talking about initiating a customer market segmentation project and you are slated to lead it.'

'So we're talking segmentation? In order to optimize marcomm?'

'Sure, and other things like product penetration.'

'I see,' Scott said. 'I just need to have a good understanding of the purpose, the strategy around segmentation. Why are we doing it?'

'We've not gone far down that road, but what does it matter? Are you talking about hiring segment managers?'

'No, it's just that if the strategy is to increase market share that requires a different hypothesis and different data than if the strategy is to increase, say, net margin. Or product bundling.'

'Or maximizing marcomm.'

He smiled. 'Right.'

She nodded. 'For now let's say the purpose is to understand and exploit differences in customer segments in order to optimize marcomm and product bundling. Does that work for you?'

He nodded. 'Yes. How much time do we have?'

She took another long sip of her coffee. 'If we get out of this what I hope to, this will generate differences in marketing communications as well as product targeting. That has implications for advertising and merchandizing.'

'Ah,' he said. 'That means a long lead time to implementation.'

'Let me worry about that. You get us actionable segments, something we can test, something that proves to senior leadership that versioning works.'

'I see. So... ?'

'Can we have a rough draft in a month or so?'

'I'll have to do some exploration, but let's aim for that.'

She smiled and he stood up and walked back to his office. Scott thought about what she said. That would be a lot of work. He sketched out a process, outputting segmentation based on consumer behaviour with the goal of understanding marcomm and product penetration. He wrote a list of steps on his white board and then invited stakeholders to a collection of meetings. They were starting a big project: customer behavioural segmentation.

Strategize

The first step in behavioural segmentation is to strategize. This tends to be a view through two lenses: marketing strategy and consumer behaviour. These two should not be contradictory.

Scott's team met and talked about the purpose of the segmentation: understanding customer preference and use for marcomm and product penetration. Scott knew in the back of his mind this probably meant doing marcomm valuation or media mix modelling by segment as well as market basket modelling by segment. It also meant he would have to investigate category management.

They needed to collect marcomm data, both from a send and a response point of view. That is, they needed to know what they sent to each customer and what the response was. They needed product-purchasing data. The question then became at what level in the product hierarchy the data collection should be undertaken. They could go down to the shop keeping unit (SKU) but that would mean 50,000 SKUs, which was way too granular. These SKUs rolled up to a higher level and these higher levels rolled up to a top level which had 6 product families, clearly too few. The team decided on a data aggregations variable called product group, which had about 30 broad product categories.

In terms of customer behaviour, Scott's team hypothesized potential customer segments. They thought there would likely be one or more generally sensitive to price, one or more having different product penetrations, one or more reacting to compelling messages designed for them and one or more that preferred one channel over another. This is just using tactical marketing (product, price, promotion and place) differentially against each segment.

The real issue was in terms of behaviour. They talked long about what caused the behaviours they would see. Things that came up included loyalty, competition, tastes and preferences, seasonality, discretionary income, etc. They needed to understand what caused lifetime value, why one segment purchased deep in a few product categories and why another segment purchased very wide product categories. If they could find differences such as these, the segmentation would be a success. The ultimate object would be to generate a portfolio of testable hypotheses. That is, a completely different communication style would be used on a price-sensitive, narrow product-purchasing consumer as opposed to an emotionally loyal price-insensitive, wide product-purchasing consumer. Scott thought there would be a lot of excitement and buy-in for this output.

Collect behavioural data

Scott went to his database team and they talked about what data they had. First, they had to define a customer (as opposed to a small business, eg a sole proprietorship) but that was fairly straightforward. Then they talked about data.

Scott wanted behavioural data, specifically transactions and marcomm responses. They talked about two or three years of history. The retail business has a strong seasonality (peaking in August and even more in December) and Scott had already learned how seasonality had to be taken into account.

They would include product details as well as gross revenue and discounts applied, net revenue, number of purchases, time between purchases, and months the product(s) were purchased.

Thinking about marcomm responses (a sign of behaviour and an indication of engagement) they talked about both direct mail and e-mail and SMS. They would mostly ignore social media/inbound marketing because of difficulty in matching customers, and web banner/advertising (again, cannot tie directly to a particular customer). They knew to whom they sent a catalogue, when they sent the catalogue, and what was on the cover and inside offers/promotions of each catalogue. Each catalogue had a unique 0800 telephone number so when the customers called, the call centre would know what (at least) catalogue drove that inquiry. If a promotion was used online those were also unique to each catalogue. The same data was available for e-mail. Each catalogue was sent to a particular e-mail address and they could keep track of each open and click. Similar (although in much less volume) was available for SMS.

Collect additional data

The next step is to collect additional data. This could come from several possible sources. It could come from creating/deriving data from the database. It could come from overlay data or from primary market research data.

From the customer database they created additional variables. These included monthly dummy variables for seasonality. They calculated time between purchases, they derived typical market baskets and they put together share of products, that is, percentage of electronics purchased, percentage of clothing purchased, percentage of office/paper products purchased, etc.

They purchased overlay data. This included both demographics (age, education, income, gender, size of household, occupation) as well as lifestyle and interest variables. They hoped these would flesh out the segments. This data is pretty well matched, at about 80 per cent to their customer database.

There was a limited amount of primary marketing research but Scott found a few studies that could be helpful. They had done a customer satisfaction study and they had done an awareness study. These studies each took customer names from the database and, while not well represented, could be matched to the transaction file.

Analytics

Collect data and sample

Note there are two kinds of variables in this process: segmenting variables and profiling variables. Segmenting variables are those used to create the segments, while profiling variables are everything else. The primary marketing research data will be profiling variables, as they are too underpopulated to be used as segmenting variables. Most of the demographics will be profiling variables, as demographics are typically not useful in defining segments. But the other (behavioural) variables will go through the algorithm and be tested as to whether or not they are significant and if so will be kept as segmenting variables. Note that anything that is not a segmenting variable will be a profiling variable.

What's next is what Scott has been most looking forward to: the analytics. There are several steps in this process and they are all enjoyable.

First, he would have to take a sample. LCA cannot operate on millions (or even hundreds of thousands) of records. The algorithm would take years to converge. So he chooses a random sample of 20,000 customer records. These records have been matched with transactions and marcomm responses, derived data and overlay data and (where possible) primary marketing research data.

Usually there is no need to worry about issues such as over-sampling (a certain variable) or stratifying. In typical consumer marketing a simple random sample is fine.

Normalize

Now, even though not strictly necessary, is the stage to weed out non-normality. This is to ensure against strange or weird data elements. There are two stages.

The first stage is simply to test every variable for 'non-normality'. This generally means taking the z-score of each variable or standardizing each variable, then deleting any observation that has a score > +/– 3.0 standard deviations. (Three standard deviations is 99.9 per cent of the observations in a normal distribution and are therefore very NON-normal.) These are clearly non-normal data elements and there should not be very many of them. Some people replace these outliers with the mean but if there are enough observations this is not necessary and a little too arbitrary.

For the second stage a common approach is to use something like K-means to test for normality. The idea is to run K-means with a LOT of clusters, perhaps 100 or so. Use the (typically behavioural) variables that make most sense to you in defining the clusters. All we are trying to do is form clusters that are unusual in terms of behavioural motivations. So now with 100 clusters, those clusters that are very small (like having only a few customers in them) are by multivariate definition 'unusual'. These observations should be eliminated. The point is that while we've looked at any single variable being unusual, this technique uses a multivariable approach to find a group of customers moving in such a way to be non-normal. That's why these observations (customers) are deleted from further analysis.

Note that we are trying to understand the normal market. That's why there is effort put into detecting non-normality. Because we have a sample it's even more important to ascertain unusual scores on variables or unusual customer behaviour and then eliminate it.

So, Scott's team went through this process and their sample went from 20,000 to 18,000. Then he randomly split this 18,000 into two files, A and B. These will be a test file and a validation file for later.

Run LCA

Now Scott feeds test file A into the software and is ready to run LCA. He first chooses to run a solution creating segments 2 to 9, just to narrow down where things are. LCA shows diagnostics (BIC, LL, etc – see Chapter 20) to help with the optimal number of segments (see Table 21.1).

Note that the BIC goes down and is at a minimum at 6 segments. This tells Scott 6 segments are probably the right number. The Bayes Information Criterion (BIC) can be thought of as an area of error (essentially negative probability) with the smaller the area the better. Whichever cluster has the smallest error (in terms of predicting membership) the better it is. Note in the first run 5 clusters seem to be the best (the smallest BIC).

TABLE 21.1   LCA first run

	BIC
3 cluster	45,506
4 cluster	41,065
5 cluster	28,655
6 cluster	29,878
7 cluster	31,556
8 cluster	38,065
9 cluster	44,005

Now he runs the second model, after deleting those variables that are insignificant and comes up with Table 21.2. The first model narrows it down to about 5 segments so he starts with 4 segments and only goes up to 8 segments. Again the BIC is lowest on 5.

TABLE 21.2   LCA second run

	BIC
4 cluster	38,556
5 cluster	37,659
6 cluster	38,005
7 cluster	39,855
8 cluster	41,066

The variables he uses also give diagnostics as to which are significant. Note Table 21.3 below, showing $R^2 < 10\%$ for most of the demographics. Scott removes these.

TABLE 21.3   Insignificant variables

AGE	0.05
EDUCATION (YEARS)	0.07
INCOME	0.01
SIZE HH	0.02
OCCUPATION – BLUE COLLAR	0.05
OCCUPATION – WHITE COLLAR	0.04
OCCUPATION – AGRICULTURE	0.02
OCCUPATION – GOVERNMENT	0.01
OCCUPATION – UNEMPLOYED	0.02
ETHNICITY – ASIAN	0.02
ETHNICITY – WHITE	0.02
ETHNICITY – BLACK	0.01

This is part of the modelling exercise: put variables in, run the segment solutions, see where BIC is best, look at significance and remove those that are insignificant. While this seems time-consuming, it ends up being far faster than, say, K-means, mostly because there is absolutely a good solution at the end, not an arbitrary quagmire of undifferentiated clusters.

The variables that end up being significant include those in Table 21.4.

Note that these variables are behavioural, as expected. The 'share of product' metric is a created variable (spend on product X out of total budget) and is usually a good indicator of (retail) behaviour. Revenue variables are not even tested, as they are the RESULT of behaviour. Demographics typically are not significant and are also not behavioural. Of course, any and all of these variables can be used for profiling.

The next step is to correct for white noise, using bivariate residuals. This step adds a large number of parameters and will slow the analysis

TABLE 21.4   Significant variables

SHARE KITCHEN APPL/COOKWARE
SHARE HOME DÉCOR
SHARE SMALL ELECTRONICS
SHARE LIVING ROOM FURNITURE
SHARE KITCHEN/DINING FURNITURE
SHARE BEDROOM FURNITURE
SHARE WOMEN'S CLOTHING/ACCESSORIES
SHARE MEN'S CLOTHING/ACCESSORIES
SHARE KID'S CLOTHING/ACCESSORIES
SHARE BABY'S CLOTHING/ACCESSORIES
SHARE JEWELLERY/WATCHES
SHARE TOYS
NUMBER EM OPEN
NUMBER EM CLICK
NUMBER PROD PURCH IN STORE
NUMBER PROD PURCH ONLINE
NUMBER DM DISCOUNT
NUMBER EM DISCOUNT
NUMBER SMS DISCOUNT
NUM ONLINE PURCH
NUM STORE PURCH
Q3 PURCHASE
Q4 PURCHASE
AVG TIME BETWEEN PURCH (MONTHS)
AVG TIME BETWEEN WEB VISITS (WEEKS)

down. Way down. Analytically, all three dimensions are nudged simultaneously: find the number of segments, find the significant variables and correct with bivariate residuals.

The next step is to mark those bivariate residuals. These are indications of some pattern remaining that the independent variables are not eliminating. The bivariate residuals should be checked down to about 3.84. This is the 95% level of confidence (remember the 95% z-score for linear models is 1.96 and 3.84 = 1.96 * 1.96, a curvilinear metric).

The common last step is to run the second file through using the same number of segments and the same variables found to be significant. Check the bivariate residuals and look at the two outputs. They should appear essentially the same. I don't usually statistically 'test' this sameness, I just look at it. I have never seen the two results to be different in any meaningful way.

Profile and output

The profile generally uses all the variables. Often there is a 'top down' view and a 'bottom up' view, or a strategy view and a tactical view, or a general view and a specific view. Table 21.5 presents the strategic, top down or general view of the five segments. This lens puts the segments together, to compare and contrast, all at once, looking at KPIs.

A few quick comments can be made on the output above. First is that some demographics are shown. This is typical. Remember that while demographics are not statistically significant in designing the segmentation, they might still be of use in fleshing out the segments. (And advertisers seem to love demographics.)

The first stage is partitioning and the second stage is probing. Adding additional data is part of the probing stage.

Let's look at the segmentation solution, Figure 21.1. Segment 1 is the largest in terms of market and each segment is successively smaller with Segment 5 the smallest at 7 per cent of the customers (on the db). The story is how segment size compares to percentage of revenue generated. Note that Segment 2 contributes 40 per cent of the revenue with only 26 per cent of the customers. Note that Segment 3, conversely, is not pulling its fair share having 19 per cent of the customers but generating only 15 per cent of the revenue. These metrics begin to let Scott know where he should put his resources and which segments are 'worth' marketing to.

TABLE 21.5   Segment KPIs

	SEG 1	SEG 2	SEG 3	SEG 4	SEG 5
% OF MARKET	33%	26%	19%	15%	7%
% OF REVENUE	17%	40%	15%	17%	11%
AVG TOTAL UNITS	14.49	25.64	8.88	18.17	7.95
SHARE KITCHEN APPLIANCES	4%	4%	1%	1%	2%
SHARE KITCHEN COOKWARE	21%	0%	2%	2%	1%
SHARE HOME DÉCOR	33%	0%	1%	1%	6%
SHARE SMALL ELECTRONICS	6%	11%	0%	3%	1%
SHARE CONSUMER ELECTRONICS	2%	31%	0%	1%	3%
SHARE LIVING ROOM FURNITURE	0%	1%	0%	0%	19%
SHARE KITCHEN FURNITURE	1%	0%	2%	0%	11%
SHARE DINING FURNITURE	0%	0%	2%	2%	21%
SHARE BEDROOM FURNITURE	4%	0%	0%	0%	18%
SHARE WOMEN'S CLOTHING	6%	0%	1%	32%	3%
SHARE WOMEN'S ACCESSORIES	12%	0%	2%	18%	2%
SHARE MEN'S CLOTHING/ACCESSORIES	7%	14%	0%	19%	4%
SHARE KID'S CLOTHING/ACCESSORIES	0%	0%	38%	9%	2%
SHARE BABY'S CLOTHING	0%	0%	12%	6%	1%
SHARE BABY'S ACCESSORIES	0%	0%	21%	1%	2%
SHARE JEWELLERY	2%	21%	0%	3%	1%
SHARE WATCHES	2%	18%	0%	1%	2%
SHARE TOYS	0%	0%	18%	1%	1%
# DM SENT	26.7	41.6	29.8	28.6	36.4
# EM SENT	66.8	87.6	55.4	41.9	44.9
# EM OPEN	11.8	64.8	49.7	9.8	8.6
# EM CLICK	2.1	33.8	35.7	3.6	7.6
# SMS SENT	11.9	55.0	44.6	32.6	24.5

TABLE 21.5   *continued*

	SEG 1	SEG 2	SEG 3	SEG 4	SEG 5
# PROD PURCH ONLINE	0.7	23.1	7.1	1.8	1.6
# PROD PURCH STORE	13.8	2.6	1.8	16.4	6.4
EDUCATION (YEARS)	11.8	21.5	11.7	17.9	13.8
MEDIAN HOUSEHOLD INCOME	60K	155K	60K	140K	20K
% Q4 PURCHASE	25%	70%	83%	14%	15%
AVG TIME BETWEEN PURCH	6.5	3.1	16.5	4.2	9.4

FIGURE 21.1   Percentage of market vs. percentage of revenue

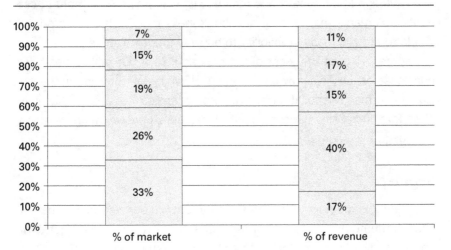

Another story displays itself around channel preference. Segments 2 and 3 seem to be very web-centric, while Segment 1 is NOT one that pursues online purchases. Segment 2 opens 64.8 of the 87.6 e-mails sent to them (>73 per cent), whereas Segment 1 opens 11.8 of the 66.8 (about 17 per cent) e-mails sent to them. Segment 2 purchases >23 of their 25.6 products online (and Segment 1 purchases <1 of their 14.49 products online). These are clear behavioural differences.

Segment 2 has the highest and Segment 5 has the lowest income. Segment 2 has the most education and Segment 3 the least education. These and other demographics can help 'flesh out' the segment profile.

Comments/details on individual segments

A few observations on each segment follow. These notes should help identify WHY each segment is a segment. Each should tell a distinct story. There should be no obvious way to 'combine' any two segments into one segment, in that each are so differentiated from each other.

Segment 1

Segment 1 is the largest segment (33 per cent of the market) and contributes 17 per cent of the revenue. This segment is clearly not pulling its fair share of revenue.

This segment seems to be product-centric around kitchen appliances, cookware and home décor. This begins to suggest a strategy. They come in on average at 6.5 weeks and they buy in a very narrow number of categories. A market basket analysis should help see which other products would tend to increase probability to buy in wider categories.

Segment 1 gets the least direct mail sent to it but makes nearly no purchases online. This may be a result of RFM usage. They are on the low side in terms of education and do not seem to be very tech savvy. Therefore, increasing direct mail (which can be expensive) might be a way to engage this segment more.

Segment 2

Segment 2 is the next to the largest segment (26 per cent of the market) and contributes more than their fair share of the revenue at 40 per cent. The strategy in place for this segment seems to be working.

It looks to be more of a men's segment that focusses on electronics and does not buy much in the store and uses e-mail and SMS. They buy a lot of watches and jewellery. Market basket analysis would reveal how to bundle. Elasticity modelling would probably show this segment to be insensitive to price since they come in so often (every 3.1 weeks), buy a lot, and have the most education and the highest income.

Segment 3

Segment 3 makes up 19 per cent of the customer market but only accounts for 15 per cent of the revenue. A strategy needs to be devised to increase the loyalty and engagement resulting in more generated revenue.

Segment 3 buys in a very narrow category range, mostly kids and baby products. This segment buys a high percentage online but they purchase more than every 16 weeks. Some 83 per cent of their purchases happen in Q4, that is, this segment buys kids and baby clothes and toys only for the holidays. As mentioned above, Segment 3 appears to be web-centric.

Segment 4

Segment 4 is 15 per cent of the market and generates 17 per cent of the revenue. This segment also buys in a rather narrow category range, mostly clothing, although it is for both men and women. Currently Segment 4 gets the fewest number of e-mails sent and media mix or marcomm valuation would help drive a vehicle/channel strategy. Given this segment's higher income they are probably insensitive to price so the strategy needs to be more compelling than merely offering discounts.

Segment 5

This is the smallest segment at only 7 per cent of the customer base but a very successful segment in terms of driving in more than their fair share of revenue at 11 per cent. This segment buys a lot in the store, so must continue to have a good in-store experience. They have by far the lowest income, at 9.4 weeks do not come into the store very often, but tend to buy a lot, mostly furniture. Obviously widening this segment's category purchases requires elasticity modelling and market basket.

Elasticity modelling

One very natural and helpful exercise after segmentation is to do elasticity modelling. (Remember Chapter 6 on demand went through the modelling detail.) This shows different price sensitivities by segment. That is, one segment will likely be sensitive to price and another segment will likely NOT be sensitive to price. This allows for very lucrative strategies.

What Scott found (see Table 21.6) was that segments 1, 3 and 5 are sensitive to price, while segments 2 and 4 are not sensitive to price. (To calculate elasticity for segment 1: PRICE COEFF * AVG N_PRICE / AVERAGE TOTAL UNITS = $-2.50 * 8.50 / 14.49 = -1.47$. Note that the absolute value is > 1.00 and thus this segment is sensitive to price, ie price elastic.)

TABLE 21.6   Elasticity calculations

	SEG 1	SEG 2	SEG 3	SEG 4	SEG 5
AVG TOTAL UNITS	14.49	25.64	8.88	18.17	7.95
AVG N_PRICE	8.50	10.75	11.25	6.50	10.00
PRICE COEFF	−2.50	−2.00	−1.25	−1.75	−3.50
ELAST	−1.47	−0.84	−1.58	−0.63	−4.40

Market basket analysis

Very strong strategy showed itself in by-segment analytics, as it usually did. This includes market basket analysis (MBA). (See Chapter 11 on logistic regression and MBA.)

The advantage of MBA by segment is the same as it always is: different segments have different sensitivities and behaviours and attacking each segment differently allows unique strategies. This gives a chance for a win–win, both to the customer and the firm.

In this case, Scott wanted to show that different segments have different product penetrations. Different segments buy products together in unique ways. That is, one size does NOT (and never will) fit all. Tables 21.7 and 21.8 show segment 1 vs. segment 5, and the same products. Typically, an MBA would be done for ALL major product categories and shown by segment.

Those customers in segment 1 that bought kitchen cookware are 123 per cent more likely to also buy home décor. Likewise, those customers in Segment 1 that bought kitchen cookware (see Table 21.7) are 44 per cent less likely to also buy kitchen furniture. This gives implications for bundling, messaging and so on.

Contrast this with customers in segment 5. These customers who bought kitchen cookware are 21 per cent less likely to also buy home décor. Likewise, those customers in segment 5 who bought kitchen cookware are 134 per cent more likely to also buy kitchen furniture. This shows the advantages of versioning say direct mail or e-mail targeting different implications by segment. The above means that bundling kitchen cookware and home décor in segment 1 makes great sense but that it is disastrous to send this same offer to customers in segment 5.

TABLE 21.7   MBA Segment 1

SEGMENT 1	KITCH COOK	HOME DÉCOR	SM ELECT	CON ELECT	LR FURN	KITCH FURN	JEWELLERY
KITCH COOK	XXX						
HOME DÉCOR	123%	XXX					
SM ELECT	45%	67%	XXX				
CON ELECT	36%	21%	87%	XXX			
LR FURN	–12%	–24%	2%	21%	XXX		
KITCH FURN	–44%	–34%	–12%	–12%	24%	XXX	
JEWELRY	23%	12%	3%	4%	–44%	–34%	XXX

TABLE 21.8   MBA Segment 5

SEGMENT 5	KITCH COOK	HOME DÉCOR	SM ELECT	CON ELECT	LR FURN	KITCH FURN	JEWELLERY
KITCH COOK	XXX						
HOME DÉCOR	–21%	XXX					
SM ELECT	–34%	–41%	XXX				
CON ELECT	3%	37%	45%	XXX			
LR FURN	78%	123%	134%	147%	XXX		
KITCH FURN	134%	67%	74%	94%	147%	XXX	
JEWELLERY	3%	14%	41%	21%	45%	67%	XXX

Scott showed these results to both the marcomm and marketing strategy teams. The product managers were impressed as well and asked Scott's team to update this analysis every quarter.

Lifetime value

Scott's team then did lifetime value (LTV) modelling on each segment using survival analysis. This was hypothesized to show what levers marketers had to change customer's lifetime value.

Of great interest was how a discount would affect segments, or what impact a decrease in price would have in terms of bringing a purchase in sooner. Table 21.9 shows the results of survival modelling focussing on the change in price coefficient.

TABLE 21.9   Survival modelling: price coefficient

	SEG 1	SEG 2	SEG 3	SEG 4	SEG 5
PRICE COEFF	−0.44	−0.25	−0.48	−0.19	−1.32
(e^B)-1	−0.36	−0.22	−0.38	−0.17	−0.73
average impact	−2.31	−0.69	−6.24	−0.72	−6.89
next TB PURCH	4.19	2.41	10.26	3.48	2.51
percentage impact	36%	22%	38%	17%	73%

Note that a change in price on segment 1 pulls in the time until purchase by 2.31 weeks and the next expected purchase in, not 6.5 weeks, but 4.19 weeks. That decrease in 2.31 weeks not only means the firm collects revenue faster but gives room for this segment to perhaps add more purchases in the year, thus increasing revenue and increasing value. Now note that segment 4 (very insensitive to price) will also respond to a price decrease but in a much less impactful way. A change to that segment will bring in the purchase by only 0.72 weeks which is 17 per cent of the previous average of 4.2 weeks.

Clearly an ROI can be calculated here (part of lifetime value) in that a cost is incurred in giving away margin but an increase results, both in velocity and amount. Obviously other marketing levers can be modelled as well, for example a change in marcomm vehicle (e-mail, direct mail, SMS, etc). Or perhaps a bundle of one product with another will cause a segment's purchases to happen faster. The point is that survival modelling not only gives a predicted time until purchase but can also show strategic levers for marketers to pull to change (increase) a customer's LTV.

Test and learn plan

The last step tends to be putting together some kind of testing plan. The idea is to corroborate the sensitivities the segmentation found. That is, if a segment is sensitive to price, test that. If a segment prefers a particular channel, test that.

Usually selection is tested first, then promotion and then channel or product category. These are usually in a test vs. control situation.

Conclusion

This chapter was meant as an example showing insights drawn from behavioural segmentation. Part of the power is to apply a different model to each segment. This can be elasticity by segment, elasticity by product/by segment, market basket by segment, lifetime value by segment, etc.

The strategy is to use the homogeneity of each segment's behaviour and sensitivities to marketing levers to exploit additional values and to treat each as a segment of one. This results in a win–win for both the firm and the customer. The customer gets just what they want, the right product offered at the right price through the right channel just when they need it and the firm gets what they want: customer satisfaction and loyalty.

Checklist

You'll be the smartest person in the room if you:

☐ Insist on doing different models for each segment, realizing this approach generates the most insights and testable options.

☐ Demand segmentation be part of the strategy process.

☐ Take advantage of each segment's preferences and sensitivities and exploit those to create a win–win for both the firm and the customer.

CREATING TARGETED 22 MESSAGES

MARKETING QUESTION

How can I create compelling messages based on product categories purchased?

ANALYTIC SOLUTION

Category management by segment

Overview

Retail and consumer packaged goods (CPG) have a number of unique features. One of them is that their products tend to be purchased routinely (unlike housing or automobiles). Another is that these industries have sub-product categories, that is, a product can be sub-divided into a smaller granularity. This means there is a 'product hierarchy' rolling up from (very detailed, granular) stock-keeping units (SKUs) to the highest, broadest level of products. These are called categories. For example, in fashion, men's blue-dyed distressed jeans might be a SKU that rolls up to a category called denim jeans.

Another difference is that customers view major product categories as fulfilling particular roles. Category management (as a strategy) comes from CPG but I'll give you a unique by-segment spin aimed at retail strategy.

CPG defines four 'roles' that customers give to product categories. A category is a distinct, managed group of products that customers perceive to be interrelated or substituted for their needs. These roles are not driven by finance, advertising or supply-side logistics but by customer behaviour.

The roles assigned to product categories (using groceries as an example) are:

- Destination: Key staples like milk, bread and meat. It is WHY shoppers visit. A large percentage of customers buy these products and they buy a large number of them.

- Occasional: Important to the shopper, mostly seasonal or based on occasion/season, eg birthday, anniversary, Christmas.

- Convenience: Purchased infrequently, but important when a customer buys them. In a grocery store these are hardware items, shoe polish, etc.

- Routine: These tend to be items like pet products, paper towels, toilet tissue. A small percentage of consumers purchase these but they buy a large number of them.

In groceries, a role is assigned to a product and it is assumed that all shoppers give that same role to the product. In retail that is not the case. This is important. Grocery stores assume all customers give, say, milk as a destination role and come to the store specifically for that. Retail assumes that different segments may assign different roles to the same product. That is, one segment may indeed go to the grocery store specifically to buy milk but another buys milk only for cooking and therefore assigns it a routine role.

Analytics can show that different segments assign a different role to the SAME category. Let's say segment X assigns the role of 'destination' to kid's clothes (it is the reason they come to the store) but segment Y assigns the role of 'seasonal' to kid's clothes. No marketing strategist would message kid's clothes the same way to each segment and that is the point.

Now, how do we determine (calculate) the assignment of these four roles by segment? There are usually two metrics that distinguish a simple lattice squares, a 2 x 2 matrix. The percentage of the segment purchasing the categorizing is on the vertical axis and the number of items (of the category) purchased is on the horizontal axis (see Figure 22.1). The four quadrants of these metrics, when comparing one segment to another, tends to differentiate and assign the roles described above. (In practice, these metrics are indexed by segment and plotted on the above metrics as axis.)

FIGURE 22.1   Category roles

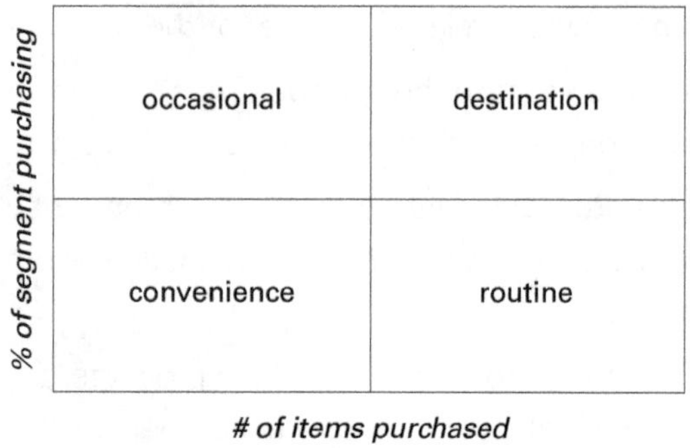

| | occasional | destination |
| % of segment purchasing | convenience | routine |

# of items purchased

Using this descriptive framework, each segment can be plotted in terms of product categories. That is, where a grocery store assumes all customers treat steak as a staple (a destination role) there may be a segment that treats steak as an occasional (even seasonal) role. This means that after segmentation has been performed each segment can be plotted and different roles can be assigned.

As an example, see Table 22.1 showing men's clothing & accessories. The metrics are 'percentage of segment purchasing' and 'average number of category units purchased by segment'. These are then indexed to the mean and plotted on the graph (Figure 22.2) after that. Note that segment 1 plots as occasionally (even seasonally) buying men's clothing & accessories whereas segment 2 calculates as assigning a destination role to men's clothing & accessories. No marketing manager would send the same messages or offers to these two segments in terms of this category.

TABLE 22.1   Category management metrics

MEN'S CLOTH / ACCESS	% PURCH	# PURCH
SEGMENT1	0.65	1.1
SEGMENT2	2.18	2.41
SEGMENT3	0.03	0.05
SEGMENT4	1.88	1.54
SEGMENT5	0.26	0.27

FIGURE 22.2   Category management metrics

Conclusion

Category management came from CPG industries. It is an approach that defines each category (major product) in terms of four different roles assigned by customers. These roles are destination, occasion, convenience and routine. The classification of these roles depends on customers scoring along two axes: percentage purchasing and number of purchases.

Take this approach one step further and do category management by segment. That is, one segment may treat a product category as a destination but another will treat that same product as convenience. This differentiation means that messages and promotions and bundling offers can be versioned by segment.

Checklist

You'll be the smartest person in the room if you:

☐ Do not treat customers with a 'one size fits all' strategy.

☐ Point out how different a segment assigning a 'destination' role is to a product category than another segment assigning an 'occasional' role to the same product category.

☐ Recommend using category management by segment as a way to create compelling versions of messages.

RFM VS. SEGMENTATION

23

MARKETING QUESTION

Why go beyond RFM?

ANALYTIC SOLUTION

Explain advantages and disadvantages of RFM

This chapter was published in a different format in
Marketing Insights, April 2014

Introduction

Whilst RFM (recency, frequency and monetary) is used by many firms, it in fact has limited marketing usage. It is really only about engagement. It is valuable for a short-term, financial orientation but as organizations grow and become more complex a more sophisticated analytic technique is needed. RFM requires no marketing strategy and as firms increase complexity there needs to be an increase in strategic planning. Segmentation is the right tool for both.

RFM has been a pillar of database marketing for 75 years. It can easily identify your 'best' customers. It works. So why go beyond RFM? To answer that, let's make sure we all know what we're talking about.

What is RFM?

One definition could be, 'An essential tool for identifying an organization's best customers is the recency/frequency/monetary formula.' RFM came about more than 75 years ago for direct marketers. It was especially popular when database marketing pioneers (Stan Rapp, Tom Collins, David Shepherd, Arthur Hughes and others) started writing their books and advocating database marketing (as the next generation of direct marketing) nearly 50 years ago. It became a popular way to make a database build (an expensive project) return a profit. Thus, the most pressing need was to satisfy finance.

Jackson and Wang wrote, 'In order to identify your best customers, you need to be able to look at customer data using recency, frequency and monetary analysis (RFM)...'. Again the focus is on identifying your best customers. But, it is not marketing's job to just identify your 'best' customers. 'Best' is a continuum and should be based on far more than merely past financial metrics.

The usual way RFM is put into place, although there are an infinite number of permutations, ends up incorporating three scores (see Table 23.1). First, sort the database in terms of most recent transactions and score the top 20 per cent, say, with a 5 and on down to the bottom 20 per cent with a 1. Then re-sort the database based on frequency, maybe with the number of transactions in a year. Again, the top 20 per cent get a 5 and the bottom 20 per cent get a 1. The last step is to re-sort the database on, say, sales dollar volume. The top 20 per cent get a 5 and the bottom 20 per cent get a 1. Now, sum the three columns (R + F + M) and each customer will have a total ranging from 15 to 3. The highest scores are the 'best' customers.

TABLE 23.1 RFM analysis of customers

CUST ID	R	F	M	TOTAL
999	3	2	1	6
1001	5	3	3	11
1003	4	4	2	10
1005	1	5	2	8
1007	1	4	1	6
1009	2	4	3	9
1010	3	4	4	11
1012	2	3	5	10
1014	3	1	5	9
1016	4	1	4	9
1017	5	2	3	10
1018	4	3	4	11
1020	4	4	3	11
1022	3	5	3	11
1024	2	4	2	8
1026	1	3	5	9

Note that this 'best' is entirely from the firm's point of view. The focus is not about customer behaviour, not about what the customer needs, why those with a high score are so involved or why those with a low score are not so engaged. The point is to make a (financial) return on the database, not to understand customer behaviour. That is, the motivation is financial and not marketing.

RFM works, as a method of finding those most engaged. It works to a certain extent, and that extent is selection and targeting. RFM is simple and easy to use, easy to understand, easy to explain and easy to implement. It requires no analytic expertise. It doesn't really even require marketers, only a database and a programmer.

Assume you rescore the database every month, in anticipation of sending out the new catalogue. That means that every month each customer potentially changes RFM value tiers. After every time period a new score is run and a new migration emerges. Note that you cannot learn why customers changed their purchasing patterns, why they decreased their buying, why they made fewer purchases or why the time between purchases changed. Much like the tip of an iceberg, only the blatant results are seen and RFM gives nothing in the way of understanding the underlying motivations that caused the resultant actions. There can be no rationale as to customer behaviour because the purpose of the algorithm used was not for understanding customer behaviour. RFM uses the three financial metrics and does not use an algorithm that differentiates customer behaviour.

Because RFM cannot increase engagement (it only benefits from whatever level of involvement, brand loyalty, satisfaction, etc you inherited at the time – with no idea WHY) it tends to make marketers passive. There is no relationship building because there is no customer understanding. That is, because RFM cannot provide a rationale as to what makes one value tier behave the way they do, marketing strategists cannot actively incentivize deeper engagement.

RFM is a good first step, but to make a great step requires something beyond RFM. Marketers require behavioural segmentation in order to practise marketing.

What is behavioural segmentation?

Behavioural segmentation (BS) quickly followed RFM, due to the frustrations that RFM produced good, but not great, results. As with most things, complex analysis requires complex analytic tools and expertise. BS was put into place to apply marketing concepts when using a database for marketing purposes.

In order to institute a marketing strategy, there needs to be a process. Kotler recommended the four Ps of strategic strategy: partition, probe, prioritize and position. Partitioning is the process of segmentation.

Whilst it's mathematically true that partitioning only requires a business rule (RFM is a business rule) to divide the market into sub-markets, behavioural segmentation is a specific analytic strategy. It uses customer behaviour to define the segments and it uses a statistical technique that maximally differentiates the segments. James H Meyers even says, 'Many people believe that market segmentation is the key strategic concept in marketing today'.

BS is from the customer's point of view, using customer transactions and marcomm response data to specifically understand what's important to customers. It is based on the marketing concept of customer-centricity. BS works for all strategic marketing activities: selection targeting, optimal price discounting, channel preference/customer journey, product penetration/category management, etc. BS allows a marketer to do more than mere targeting.

An important point might be made here. Behaviours are caused by motivations, both primary and experiential. Behaviours are purchases, visits, product usage and penetration, opens, clicks and marcomm responses. These behaviours cause financial results, revenue, growth, lifetime value, and margin.

Primary motivations would be unseen things like attitudes, tastes and preferences, lifestyle, value set on price, channel preferences, benefits, and need arousal. There are experiential, secondary causes of behaviour, typically based on some brand exposure. These are not behaviours, but cause subsequent behaviours. These secondary causes would be things like loyalty, engagement, satisfaction, courtesy, or velocity. Note that RFM uses recency and frequency, which are metrics of engagement, which is a secondary cause. RFM also uses monetary metrics which are resultant financial measures. Thus RFM does not use behavioural data, but engagement and financial data. These are very different to behavioural data used in BS. One simple way to distinguish behavioural data from secondary data is that behaviours are nouns: purchases, responses, etc, whilst secondary causes are adjectives: *engagement* metrics, *loyal* customers, *recent* transactions, *frequently* purchased.

BS typically requires analytic expertise to implement. Behavioural segmentation is a statistical output.

One critical difference between BS and RFM is that, in a behavioural segmentation, members typically do not change groups. That is, the behaviour that defines a segment evolves very slowly. For example, if one person is sensitive to price, her defining behaviour will not really change.

She is sensitive to price even after she has a baby, she is sensitive to price as she ages, or if she gets a puppy, or buys a new house. Her products purchased might change, her interests in certain campaigns might change, but her defining behaviour will not change. This is one of the advantages of BS over RFM. This is what drives your learning about the segments. BS provides such insights that each segment generates a rationale, a story, as to why it's unique enough to BE a segment.

Whilst RFM uses only three dimensions, BS uses any and all behavioural dimensions that best differentiate the segments. It typically requires far more than three variables to optimally distinguish a market.

Because marketing mix testing can be done on each segment (using product, price, promotion and place) the insights generated make for differentiated marketing strategies for each segment. To test if RFM tiers drive behaviour is probably inappropriate, because tier membership potentially changes every time period. Much like studies that proclaim, 'Women who smoke give birth to babies with low birth weight', there is spurious correlation going on. Just as another dimension (socio-economic, culture, etc) might be the real (unseen) cause of the low birth weight and NOT necessarily (only) the smoking, so there are other dimensions of (unseen) behaviour using RFM to explain campaign responses. That is, the response is not caused by the RFM tier, but some other motivation.

In short, BS goes far beyond RFM. The insights and resultant strategies are typically worth it.

What does behavioural segmentation provide that RFM does not?

BS delivers a cohort of segment members that are maximally differentiated from other segment members. Because these members typically do not change segments, various marketing strategies can be levelled at each segment to maximize cross-sell, up-sell, ROI, margin, loyalty, satisfaction, etc.

BS identifies variables that optimally define each segment's unique sensitivities. For instance, one segment might be defined by channel preference, another by price sensitivity, another by differing product penetrations and another by a preferred marcomm vehicle. This knowledge, in and of itself, generates vast insights into segment motivations. These insights allow for a differentiated positioning of each segment based on each segment's key differentiators. You get away from trying to incentivize customers out of the 'bad' tiers and into the 'good' tiers. In BS, there are no good or bad tiers. Your job is now to understand how to maximize each segment based on what drives each segment's behaviour, rather than focus on only migration. Thus, BS gives you a test-and-learn plan.

Because of the insights provided, knowledge is gained of each segment's prime pain points, which means that each segment can be treated with the right message, at the right time, with the right offer and at the right price. This kind of positioning creates a 'segment of one' in the customer's mind. This uniqueness differentiates the firm, perhaps even to the extent to move it away from heavy competition and toward monopolistic competition. This means you approach a degree of market power, that is, becoming a price maker.

Because BS provides such insights it tends to make marketers very active in understanding motivations. This tends to generate very lucrative strategies for each segment.

Conclusion

What are the advantages of RFM? It's fast, simple and easy to use, explain and implement. What are the disadvantages of behavioural segmentation? It requires analytic expertise to generate, is more costly and takes longer to do.

BS uses behavioural variables and uses them for the purpose of understanding customer behaviour and it uses a statistical algorithm to maximally differentiate each segment based on behaviour. As mentioned, the vast majority of marketers that evolve from RFM to BS say it's worth it, and their margins agree.

Checklist

You'll be the smartest person in the room if you:

- ☐ Accept the idea that RFM is a firm-centric and not a customer-centric point of view.

- ☐ Insist that segmentation be from the customer's point of view.

- ☐ Remember that RFM gives no marketing strategy and no marketing insights.

MARKETING STRATEGY

24

Customers not competitors

MARKETING QUESTION

What organizing philosophy should I use to solidify my marketing point of view?

ANALYTIC SOLUTION

Customer-centricity

Customer-centricity

There are many potential orientations or philosophies for analytics to take. There could be a firm-centric approach, or a financial orientation, a product focus, or a technology point of view.

The approach of this book (especially under the umbrella of marketing strategy) is a consumer- (most often a customer-) centric one. That's because marketing strategy is all about understanding customer behaviour and incentivizing customer behaviour in such a way that the firm wins and the customer wins.

I know a lot of marketers are saying, 'But what about competitors? Are they not part of marketing strategy?' And the answer is, 'No, not really.' I am aware of the gasps this will cause.

By understanding customer behaviour, part of that insight will come from what experience customers have with competitors, but the focus is on customer, not competitive, behaviour. I know John Nash and his work in game theory takes a back seat in this view and that is on purpose.

Just to be clear, marketing science should be at the customer level, NOT the competitive level. By focussing on competitors you automatically move from a marketing point of view toward a financial or economic point of view.

In Marketing, the Customer is Central.

A marketing orientation is customer-centric, anything else is by definition NOT marketing. Marketing drives financial results and in order to be marketing-oriented there must be a customer-centric focus. That means all marketing activities are geared to learn and understand customer behaviour.

The marketing concept does not mean giving the customer (only) what they want, because: 1) the customer's wants can be widely divergent; 2) the customer's wants may contradict the firm's minimum needs; and 3) the customer might not know what they want. It is marketing's job to learn and understand and incentivize customer behaviour to a win–win position.

So far we have focussed on customer behaviour. Marketing, to be marketing, is about understanding and incentivizing customer behaviour in a way that consumers get what they want and firms get what they want. Customers want a product that they need when they need it at a price that gives them value through a channel they prefer. Firms want loyalty, customer satisfaction and growth. Since a market is a place where buyers and sellers meet, marketing is the function that moves the buyers and sellers toward each other. The customer is the agent that makes this take place so of course great emphasis should be on the customer.

Given the above, it should be noted that much of marketing strategy has evolved (primarily via microeconomics) to a firm vs. firm rivalry. That is, marketing strategy is in danger of forgetting the focus on customer behaviour and jumping deep into something like 'game theory' wherein one firm competes with another firm, as if the firm is the acting agent. Because the firm is a collection of individuals there could not possibly be a singular acting principal to understand, incentivize, etc.

Everything that follows about marketing strategy can be thought of as an indirect consequence of firm vs. firm based on a direct consequence of focussing on customer behaviour. That is, combatting a firm means understanding and incentivizing customers. Think of it as an iceberg: what is seen (firms competing) is above the surface, but what is really happening that moves the iceberg is what is unseen (from other firms' points of view) below the surface (customers acting and responding).

Customer behaviour replaces game theory

Stephan Sorger's excellent *Marketing Analytics* has a brief description of competitive moves, both offensive and defensive. Below are summaries of each move but applied via customer behaviour.

Defensive reactions to competitor moves

- *Bypass attack* (the attacking firm expands into one of our product areas) and the correct counter is for us to constantly explore new areas. Are you familiar with Theodore Levitt's *Marketing Myopia*? If not, have a read.

- *Encirclement attack* (the attacking firm tries to overpower us with larger forces) and the correct counter is to message how our products are superior/unique and of more value. This requires a constant monitoring of message effectiveness.

- *Flank attack* (the attacking firm tries to exploit our weaknesses) and the correct counter is to not have any weaknesses. This again requires monitoring and messaging the uniqueness/value of our products.

- *Frontal attack* (the attacking firm aims at our strength) and the correct counter is to attack back in the firm's territory. Obviously this is a rarely used technique.

Offensive actions

- *New market segments*: this uses behavioural segmentation (see Chapters 19 and 20 on segmentation) and incentivizes customer behaviour for a win–win relationship.

- *Go-to-market approaches*: this learns about customers' preferences in terms of bundling, channels, buying plans, etc.

- *Differentiating functionality*: this approach extends customers' needs by offering product and purchase combinations most compelling to potential customers.

Conclusion

The overarching point is that marketing science (and marketing research and marketing strategy) should all be focussed on customer (and overall consumer) behaviour. Good marketing is customer-centric. Have you heard that before?

Marketing science is important and offers incredible value. Those analysts that do marketing science need a right view, a theory of causality for providing insights. An insight is not an observation (72 per cent of our customers enter our store wearing jeans.) An insight is something new, that explains customer behaviour and provides a competitive advantage. There must be financial implications following an insight.

My preceding book, *Marketing Analytics*, was geared at arming analysts with tools and techniques to accomplish marketing analytics. This final chapter of this book was designed as an organizing philosophy within which to operate. Now that you have all that, it's time to get to work.

REFERENCES AND FURTHER READING

Cox, D (1972) Regression models and life tables, *Journal of the Royal Statistical Society*

Cox, E (2011) *Retail Analytics: The secret weapon*, Wiley

Franks, W (2012) *Taming the Big Data Tidal Wave*, Wiley

Franks, W (2014) *The Analytics Revolution*, Wiley

Grigsby, M (2002) Modeling elasticity, *Canadian Journal of Marketing Research*, vol. 20 (2)

Grigsby, M (2015) *Marketing Analytics: A practical guide to real marketing science*, Kogan Page

Grigsby, M (2015) Analytic choices about pricing insights, *Marketing Insights Magazine*, April

Kennedy, P (1998) *A Guide to Econometrics*, MIT Press

Lewis, R and Dart, M (2010) *The New Rules of Retail: Competing in the world's toughest market place*, St Martin's Press

Marr, B (2015) *Big Data: Using smart big data, analytics and metrics to make better decisions and improve performance*, Wiley

O'Neill, D, Gerst, S and Prom, S (2014) *Business Insights: How to find and effectively communicate golden nuggets in retail data*, Delta Publishing

Pearson, B (2012) *The Loyalty Leap*, Portfolio Press

Reichheld, FF (1996) *The Loyalty Effect*, Harvard Business School Press

Siegel, E (2013) *Predictive Analytics*, Wiley

Sorger, S (2013) *Marketing Analytics: Strategic models and metrics*, Admiral Press

Stephens, D (2013) *The Retail Revival*, Wiley

Tobin, J (1958) Estimation of relationships for limited dependent variables, *Econometrica*

Venkatesan, R, Farris, P and Wilcox, RT (2015) *Cutting Edge Marketing Analytics*, Pearson Education

Vriens, M (2012) *The Insights Advantage: Knowing how to win*, iUniverse, Inc

Weinstein, A (1994) *Market Segmentation*, Irwin Professional Publishing

INDEX

Note: The index is filed in alphabetical, word-by-word order. Numbers and acronyms are filed as spelt out. Page locators in *italics* denote information contained within a Figure or Table.

CPSIA information can be obtained
at www.ICGtesting.com
Printed in the USA
JSHW011931130223
37656JS00007B/642

9 780749 477158